TRUTH VIBRATIONS

Truth Vibrations

DAVID ICKE

(Revised Edition)

Gateway

Gateway
an imprint of
Gill & Macmillan Ltd
Hume Avenue, Park West
Dublin 12
with associated companies throughout the world
www.gillmacmillan.ie

1 85860 006 5

First published 1991 by The Aquarian Press
Revised edition 1993 by Gateway

Cover design by Studio B of Bristol
Text illustrations by Jackie Morris
Text set in Bembo 10.5 on 12.5 by
MetraDisc of Castelton, Rochdale
Printed in Malaysia

*The paper used in this book comes from the wood pulp of managed
forests. For every tree felled, at least one tree is planted,
thereby renewing natural resources.*

A catalogue record is available for this book
from the British Library.

7 9 11 10 8

Contents

Introduction

As I write these opening words I am already well aware of what the reaction to this book might land up being. People reading it will probably fall into one of three main categories: those who laugh; those who condemn; and those for whom it will change their lives forever. And with every month and year that passes, the latter group will grow and grow until it is the largest.

The transformation of humankind is upon us, and there is nothing more urgent for humanity, I would most strongly suggest, than to listen to the message that is set before you here. It is impossible to overstate that urgency. The earth and all the life she supports is in the process of changes of an incomprehensible magnitude. Nothing and no one will be the same again. The earth is moving on to the next stage of her evolution, and new energies, new vibrations, are beginning to encircle the planet. The changes began in the mid-1960s, and the volume is about to be turned up rapidly through the 1990s and beyond.

As the vibrations have quickened, so have they changed the thinking of millions, and humanity is being divided into those who are tuning in and those who are not; those who are evolving at a fast speed and those stuck in the delusions of the material world. I have called these new energies Truth Vibrations, because they will affect – are affecting – our consciousness and understanding in such a way that we will open our eyes to the truths about God and life, truths which have been forgotten for so long.

This book will explain how you can tune in to these higher energies and how we, as a human race, can reduce the impact of the physical events the earth is due to undergo. There is much we can do for ourselves and the planet, but we must start now. To do this, however, will require a gigantic leap in human consciousness. We will have to let go of our old beliefs and perceptions in the face of the spiritual truths.

You can appreciate the scale of that leap when I tell you that these truths have been given to me by some of the most evolved beings in this solar system. We are not alone or even nearly alone. Every planet and star is pulsating with life, and we on earth in physical bodies are only a tiny part of the wonder that is Creation. Forgetting these truths has produced a world consumed by the emotion of fear. We fear death, we fear life, we fear today, we fear tomorrow. There is no need! There really is nothing to fear but fear itself. There is no such thing as death, and no matter what happens to us during our short visit to earth, we simply go back from whence we came. After a while our souls return in another physical body, usually in different circumstances, to learn more lessons and gain more experience in order to speed our evolution. Life is not for a few years on this planet. It is forever.

Crazy? A candidate for the funny farm? Many will think so, and I can understand this, given the way we are conditioned to believe whatever may be the prevailing 'wisdom' of the time. But it will not be many years before those who cling on to current thinking will be the ones labelled 'crazy'. Remember how they ridiculed those who said the earth was round? It is this scale of transformation that human perception is about to undergo, and it will happen, not over centuries, but over the next few years, to the end of this decade.

I could have written this book in a different way and made it an exercise in laughter-limitation. I could have ignored the more fantastic experiences that challenge belief, but that is not what I have chosen to do, nor what I have been asked to do. I have set out exactly what has happened to me and what I have been told. All the information in these pages has come through psychic communications or been confirmed as accurate by those communications. They have been passed on through many mediums and sensitives, most of whom had no idea what others had already told me, nor even knew of their existence. Some of the names of people involved in this story have been changed to protect them and their work. Where full names have been given they are correct.

The energy I have termed the Truth Vibrations has a specific role to play in the transformation of human thought. It has been 'commissioned' to take the spiritual truths out of the shadows, off the fringes, and onto the centre stage of debate. Once there, these truths cannot fail to triumph because they provide the only credible explanation for the meaning of life.

I hope the traditional churches will hear this message in the way it is given. I do not point out misunderstanding with any sense of malice or condemnation. Such emotions are of no value. But too many of the major church movements have allowed dogma to turn thinking into heresy, and it is time that was peacefully challenged. As Albert Schweitzer said: "It will ever remain incomprehensible that our generation, so great in its achievements of discovery, could be so low spiritually as to give up thinking".

If nothing else, this book will make you think. I don't ask you to believe what you read. I don't even urge you to do so. That is your choice and yours alone. But if you open your mind, the message cannot fail to open your heart. When that happens you will learn much truth, and that truth will set you free.

December 1990

In this new Gateway edition I have made few changes to the original text for two reasons. Firstly, I feel that it still represents the basis of my understanding, although the detail is evolving all the time as my consciousness expands. Secondly, this book was written at the start of my conscious awakening and it will be interesting for people who read my later books to see how the process of awakening and understanding develops and expands.

One major change, however is in my understanding of the nature of Jesus' mission, in chapter 8.

I want to make it quite clear that I do not recommend any specific psychics or counsellors who are mentioned in this book. Readers must make up their own minds about who they seek for advice.

David Icke
Isle of Wight
December 1993

1

Guided by the Light

I had felt for some months that I was being guided. I couldn't hear a voice or anything like that, I just had an overwhelming feeling that I was not alone as I journeyed through life.

And what a life it had been already. I was a professional footballer until rheumatoid arthritis ended my career, then a journalist and television presenter, before moving into politics as a national spokesperson for Britain's Green Party. There was a definite pattern emerging. I would go for something, achieve it, leave it, and move on to the next goal, the next experience. It wasn't that I consciously wanted to jump from career to career, experience to experience – circumstances dictated the sequence.

My rise to prominence in the Green Party was rapid, to the point of being ridiculous. From joining the Green Party to being elected a national spokesperson took a mere six months, and it was at this point that I became convinced that I was being led by forces beyond my understanding. Something strange was going on.

For most of my life I had never thought much about what happens after what we call death, or if there were anything for us beyond this sphere known as Planet Earth. The teachings of the traditional Church made little sense to me, and so the spiritual side of things passed me by. But the deeper I travelled into Green politics, the more it became a spiritual journey. I was soon asking many questions about the reason for our existence. Why were we here? What happened next? I wrote a book on Green issues, published in February 1990, called *It Doesn't Have To Be Like This*, and by then I was certain there were other dimensions to the universe and ourselves which we could not yet comprehend. In the chapter called 'Summon the Spirit' I wrote:

> We are not consumption machines. We have a soul. It is our soul, our life-force deep within us, call it what you like, that has been suppressed, often extinguished, by the demands of the system which denies the existence of anything that can't be seen or touched, that can't make money.

It was hardly the deepest insight into the meaning of life, but it was indicative of a fundamental change in my thinking which had been going on for a year or two, and the pace of that change was about to lift me on to a new level of understanding and knowledge. Life would never be the same again. Part of the publicity tour for the Green book included a public meeting and interviews in Nottingham, and I stayed with a couple who believed they, too, were being guided by spirits. We talked for a couple of hours that evening and I found it fascinating. At one point the husband jumped from his chair, picked up a book from the shelf, and said: "I've been told to give you this." "Who told you?" I asked innocently. "A spirit message", he replied.

I took the book with me and could not put it down. It was the writings of a medium recounting her experiences, and by now there was no question in my mind that there was much more to the universe than science had yet had the breadth of vision to discover or even perceive. What you don't look for you have little chance of finding; for centuries science has been a closed mind to these possibilities. This feeling of being guided had become intense, and I remember one night in a hotel room saying out loud, "For goodness' sake if you are there, contact me. This is driving me up the wall".

Then, one Saturday in early 1990, I went down to the sea-

front near my home to play football with my eight year old son
Gareth. On the way I bought a book called *The End of Nature*,
which I intended to read that weekend. I still haven't read it.
After football we wandered along to the sea-front railway station to have some lunch at a little cafe there, but it was full and
we began to walk away into the town to find another place to
eat. As we left the station area, I was stopped by one of the
railway staff who wanted to chat about a football match being
played that afternoon. We talked for a few minutes and I realised
Gareth was missing. He was nowhere to be seen, and the only
place he could be was in the station newsagents. I walked in and
there he was, looking at a book about railways. "Come on
Gareth", I said, "Let's go and have some lunch".

At that moment I had this tremendous urge to look at the
paperback books on the far side of the shop. Why, I had no idea;
they were usually romantic novels and such like, hardly my
scene, and I had £13 worth of book already in my hand. The last
thing I needed was another. But the urge, the compulsion to go,
was too strong to resist, and as I reached the first rack I saw a
face smiling at me from the cover of a book called *Mind to Mind*.
The face was that of Betty Shine. She is a medium and healer, a
brilliant one, as I was to learn. I had never heard the name
before, but I bought the book without a second's hesitation.

Within twenty-four hours I had read her book, and first
thing Monday morning I found her business address and wrote
asking to meet her. The book was honest, simple, and totally
credible in its explanations of how the physical body is only a
vehicle we use to exist on this physical plane of life. Our spirit-
soul simply went on to another plane of existence when the
physical body died. The body we see may die, but we go on
forever. She told of how the spirits of people formerly on earth
contacted her through voice, telepathy or vision, and it confirmed this idea of spirit guidance which I was sure was happening to me.

Betty rang a few days later, and we arranged to meet for a
session of healing. I had suffered with the arthritis since I was a
teenager, and I saw this as a chance to ease the pain. But that was
not my real motivation. I wanted to know for sure if I was
linked up with a being or force from another dimension of life.

Betty had had many psychic experiences as a child, but it was only at the age of 45 that she realised she had healing powers. She went to a medium as a last resort when doctors failed to cure a chronic health problem; she thought she was dying. The medium told her she was ill because she was born to be a spiritual healer, and there was a buildup of energy within her body that was causing the ill-health. If she wanted to be well, she had to be a healer, so that this energy could be released through her hands to her patients. She took his advice, and the moment she started healing, her health problem disappeared.

My first two visits to her were without incident, though my joints became less painful and my understanding of life expanded enormously. Visit number three, however, was to change my life. The date was Thursday, March 29th, 1990. I lay on the couch in her little healing room as she worked on my joints as usual. I can't explain what I began to sense, except that the atmosphere in the room became charged, almost thicker somehow. You could almost see the energy. I began to search for a hair I thought I could feel on my cheek, but I found nothing. I remembered reading in *Mind to Mind* that when spirits are trying to 'lock in' to our consciousness, it can feel like a spider's web has been laid across your face.

At that moment Betty said: "I'm being told you have two cats, and one of then has stomach trouble and diarrhoea. You might have to change her diet for a while." The cats had been with us for only a short time. I rang my wife Linda later that day, and she said there was no sign of anything amiss with either of them. By the time I arrived home the following after-noon, however, one was clearly suffering from stomach trouble and diarrhoea.

A few seconds after the advice about the cats, Betty visibly shuddered. "Oh", she said, "This is powerful – I'll have to close my eyes for this one!" She described the vision before her as someone of immense power. He was Chinese in appearance, and the description of his dress was subsequently confirmed as that of a mandarin. He said his last life on earth was around AD 1200 – the right time for such a costume. He gave his name as Wang Yee Lee and added "Socrates is with me". Over the next ten minutes Betty paraphrased the astonishing information

Wang was asking her to pass on to me:

There will be great earthquakes. These will come as a warning to the human race. They will occur in places that have never experienced them. Taking oil from the seabed is destabilising the inner earth. The centre of the earth will move and the poles will change. The sea spirits will rise and stop men taking oil. The sea will reclaim the land, and humans will see they cannot do these terrible things. They cannot abuse the elements. They have to be treated with respect.

In the country in which he (that is, me) lives there will be a cultural revolution in five years' time. He was chosen as a youngster for his courage. He has been tested and has passed all the tests. He was led into football to learn discipline and training, but when that was learned it was time to move on. He also had to learn how to cope with disappointment, experience all the emotions, and how to get up and get on with it. The spiritual way is tough, and no one makes it easy.

He is a healer who is here to heal the earth, and he will be world-famous. He will face enormous opposition, but we will always be there to protect him. He is still a child spiritually, but he will be given spiritual riches. Sometimes he will say things and wonder where they came from. They will be our words. Knowledge will be put into his mind, and at other times he will be led to knowledge.

We know he wanted us to contact him, but the time was not right. He was led here to be contacted, not to be cured. But one day he will be completely cured. He will always have what he needs, but no more. He should not worry about cars – electric cars will be used in eight years' time. In twenty years there will be a different kind of flying machine, very different from the aircraft of today. Time will have no meaning. Where you want to be, you will be. When he is at home, he must do family things and keep the family unit together (I had been away constantly working for television or the Green Party).

Wang Yee Lee ended the communication with the words: "If he abuses the gifts, the gifts shall be taken away".

"What an honour", Betty said, "I've never had anyone through of that power before".

I wasn't surprised at being contacted. It was a relief that I hadn't been imagining it all. But the source of the guidance and the messages left me stunned. Socrates was of course a man of rare wisdom. A philosopher in ancient Greece who died in 399 BC, he was charged with corrupting the young (by telling them truth), and after one of the most famous trials in history he was sentenced to death by drinking hemlock. He had the chance to escape and live in exile, but he refused. He talked of the divine voice that was guiding him, and he knew far more about the ways of the spiritual universe than modern science knows to-day. Souls often take on the name and form of their last or most famous life on earth when they make themselves known to us, and the souls that were once in the physical bodies of Socrates and Wang Yee Lee are now on the high spiritual planes that guide and supervise life on this planet.

Four days after I was contacted, I turned on the television news and heard of an earthquake centred on Bishops Castle near the Welsh-English border, which had affected a large area. People ran from buildings in panic, and one witness later told me how he saw an office block swaying as its occupants ran screaming into the street. The quake measured 4.9 on the Richter scale, big for Britain. It was a rather chilling experience to look at the screen, given what had happened to me I didn't believe in coincidences anymore.

The next day I was getting ready to catch the ferry to the mainland from my home on the Isle of Wight. There wasn't much time to spare, but I suggested I take my wife Linda for a quick lunch at a health food shop and cafe five minutes away. We had to rush, but I was keen to go. While she was organising the food, I felt compelled to walk over to the shop's display of books. The feeling was the same as in the newsagent's. I saw nothing to interest me and I was about to sit down again when something in my mind urged me to look on the other side of the display, which was one of those units that spin around. There my eyes caught the word... earthquake. It was an American book called *We Are The Earthquake Generation* – a rare book in the UK, it would appear, at least at this time. None of the many people I have since told about it have been able to find a copy. I was obviously interested in anything about earthquakes, but only when I saw mention of psychics did I begin to realise its significance.

"Knowledge will be put into his mind", I thought, "And at other times he will be led to knowledge".

The book was written by Jeffrey Goodman, an open-minded American scientist. He went to American psychics with proven records of accurate prediction – people like Aron Abrahamsen – and asked them independently of each other how they saw the future. Almost to the detail they predicted the same things. He added into his study the predictions of two of history's most famous psychics, Nostradamus and Edgar Cayce (pronounced *Caysee*). Nostradamus was a Frenchman born in 1503. He made many miraculous forecasts, including that of the Great Fire of London, the rise of Hitler and the work of the scientist Louis Pasteur, whom he named specifically. This, remember, was all predicted in the 16th century. Nostradamus said his prophecies were the result of linking into the 'divine source', by going into a trance. This was much the same technique as that used by Edgar Cayce, an American who became known as 'The Sleeping Prophet'. Once Cayce was in his trance he would advise, accurately, on medical conditions, and reveal details of people's previous lives, and why they had come to earth this time. When he died in 1945, he had completed a staggering 14,000 of these readings.

Both of these men predicted massive geological activity in the run-up to the year 2000. Other proven psychic prophets came to the same conclusion in Goodman's book, and they showed a highly developed knowledge of geological principles in their psychic state – knowledge which they did not otherwise possess. They predicted that in some areas land would be lost, while in others it would rise from the sea. This would bring confirmation of the existence of the so-called mythical worlds of Atlantis and Mu, or Lemuria as it is also known. I was already certain in my own mind that these places had existed, and this was later to be confirmed. The psychics said that all these events would lead up to the year 2000, when the earth would slip off its present axis.

The biggest earthquake thus far recorded by instruments had reached 8.6 on the Richter scale, but these superquakes would be more like 10 or 12, the book said. The power of a quake, as registered by Dr Charles Richter's calculations, goes up substantially with each point of the scale. It means that a quake of the magnitude of 12 can be nearly 5,000 times more powerful than one of 8.4, depending on how close to the surface it occurs. A shallow quake will concentrate its power and damage in a small area. A deeper one will disperse its power over a wider area, and while more places are affected, the damage to any specific area is less severe.

Let me make clear that I am not saying that every detail these psychics predicted in this book will come to pass, indeed I know that some of what they have mentioned has already changed for the better, and *will* continue to do so if we do what is necessary. As I have said already and will expand upon later, the severity of these events is partly up to us. I can only say that I was led to the book because its basis is correct and, as things stand now, there is going to be immense geological activity in this decade.

Here I was in possession of this information, basic as it was, but I had no idea what I was meant to do with it. I rang someone I respected in the Church of England for his advice. I feel the traditional Church as an organisation has let down the world badly with its dogma and rigidity, but there are many wonderful people within its ranks. The person I rang is one of these. He has an open mind and a genuine compassion and kindness of spirit. He listened to my story and was not in the least bit fazed by it. He asked me to call him again when we could talk further. He said it sounded very much like the messages to the Old Testament prophets Isaiah and Jeremiah, but he advised me to "eke it out gradually" without revealing the source, rather than coming out with it all. He was aware of the predictable public reaction.

I decided to take his advice: at this stage, without further information, it was sensible to put the message in the public arena without putting myself on the line. The following Sunday

I appeared on breakfast television to talk about the environment, and the same afternoon I delivered the closing speech to
the Green Party Spring Conference. I used both opportunities to
question the wisdom of taking oil from the seabed, and I predicted a period of great geological instability.

Soon after this the 'eye' appeared. One evening I was lying
on my bed in a hotel room when I closed my eyes and there,
forming out of the darkness, was the shape of an eye. It was
there for a split second at first before dispersing, but gradually it
became permanent. Within a week I was seeing eyes wherever I
looked! Betty Shine had said in her book that she experienced
the same thing. She said it was a sign that psychic powers were
developing. Why this takes the form of an eye will become
apparent. I was also led to a stream of books, some by Edgar
Cayce. If I was reading a book that was not approved in this
way, I found it a real struggle. When it was one I was meant to
read, I went through it very quickly.

I made two appointments to visit Betty Shine again, but
both had to be cancelled for different reasons. This was to
become a regular pattern. I was only meant to see her when
higher powers wanted me to see her. When we did get together
again there was another communication from Wang Yee Lee.
He began with the words "Let there be light and there was
light" and these are the messages that followed, as reported by
Betty:

Don't try to do it all alone. Go hand in hand with others so
you can pick each other up as you fall.

One man cannot change the world, but one man can communicate the message that can change the world.

The written word will be there forever. The spoken word
disappears on the wind. (Wang lifted his hand in a sort of
wafting movement as he said this.)

He will write five books in three years.

Politics is not for him. He is too spiritual. Politics is anti-spiritual and it will make him very unhappy.

He will leave politics. He doesn't have to do anything. It will happen gradually over a year.

He will leave the Isle of Wight. He will find closed minds there. It will become difficult for people who need to see him to get to the island, and he will leave.

This will take the fear away from his eldest child. She is living in fear and this is affecting her health and life, though she tries to hide it.

This last message referred to Kerry, my daughter. Betty Shine had no idea what it meant and had no way of knowing. It was about the terror Kerry has of travelling in ships, even the 40 minutes between the island and the mainland. She confirmed that the fear was indeed badly affecting her, as she worried about her next trip on the water.

One other incident happened during that second communication from Wang Yee Lee, which left me even more astonished, if that is possible. About half way through he said: "The spirit of the book he is reading is suffering great anguish. It is in his suitcase lying against a newspaper. The book is much troubled about a story in the paper about Bovine Spongiform Encephalopathy, and there is an article in the paper written by someone who is not of our kind". In the corner of the room was my briefcase, which had not been opened since I arrived, nor had I left the room at any time. Once the other messages were through, Betty said she was being told again about the book, and I went over to open the briefcase. The book I was reading was *Original Blessings*, by the American Dominican Priest, Matthew Fox, and it was lying on top of a story in that morning's paper about Bovine Spongiform Encephalopathy, better known as Mad Cow Disease. At the back of the paper was an article by a journalist who had written some particularly hostile comments about me some months before, and he could, I suppose, have fitted the bill as 'someone who is not of our kind'.

As I was to learn, everything has a spirit, and we pass on

our own spiritual vibration to everything we create. This book contains my spirit passed on through the thoughts that formed together to write it, and every single copy printed, whether my physical body is alive or dead, will carry my spirit. Amazing? Of course it is, but in this case we are not working within the limitations of thinking that we currently impose on ourselves, and have imposed upon us, in this world of physical matter. We are dealing with the real potential of humankind.

These latest messages answered many questions. I knew what I was to do with the information. I was to reveal it in books along with the spiritual truths that will transform human understanding. 'One man cannot change the world, but one man can communicate the message that can change the world'. It was going to be a privilege, but a tough one. My spiritual education, under the guidance of master souls, was showing me with every page and communication what was meant by "He was chosen as a youngster for his courage". What I was going to say in the books would indeed, in the short term, bring "enormous opposition" and much hilarity and ridicule.

By now, however, I had no doubts that I was dealing with the truth, and that, frankly, is all that matters.

2

Life After Life

It is clear that traditional views of God and the ways of the universe are fundamentally flawed.

I was led to one book after another about reincarnation and the journey of the soul through successive earth lives. I also read constantly of a law called *karma*, which explains so much that we usually think of as arbitrary 'luck' with no pattern or reason to it. How many people say, "Why me? Why do I always have the bad luck? Why am I in these circumstances? What is it all for? What is the meaning of my life?" The conventional Church can offer few answers which the vast majority will or can be expected to accept, and the spiritual side of our lives has been neglected as a consequence.

Reincarnation was the basis of early Christianity, with the writings of men like Origen, and it has always been a foundation of the Eastern religions such as Hinduism and Buddhism. The teachings of Jesus outlined the laws of reincarnation, and how our thoughts and actions in one life will decide what happens in future lives. 'What you sow, so you shall reap' was a superb summary of this law of cause-and-effect called *karma* – a Sanskrit word meaning action. Everything we do we answer for, or benefit from, in this life or those yet to come. So what

we are is what we have been, and what we do is what we will
be. Perfect justice. The Old Testament's 'An eye for an eye, a
tooth for a tooth' doesn't mean that we should all take equal
retribution for the wrongs done to us, though that is the way it
has been understood. It means karma, the law that ensures that
no one can escape the consequences of their behaviour; and if we
take our own retribution we will have to face the consequences
of that, also.

What a different complexion this puts on the world around
us! All those terrorists, hit-men, mafia bosses, fraudsters, mur-
derers, rapists and racists who believe they are getting away
with their actions if they elude the human law are being mon-
itored every second of their lives by the spiritual law. They are
shaping their destiny in this life and future lives with every
thought and deed. The terrorist might be terrorised and the
racist may return as a member of the race he or she so despises.
An Israeli could return as an Arab and an Arab an Israeli. A
Catholic could come back as a Protestant, and a white South
African as a black. How absurd human behaviour looks from
this perspective! We experience many types of existence, race,
colour and creed in our earth lives, and this makes a nonsense of
racism and religious bigotry. They are all opportunities to learn
and experience, and it is not for any of us to stand in judgment
of each other, or think of ourselves as superior. God doesn't
judge, so how can we?

We have to lose our obsession with the physical and the
material. It isn't wealth that matters - it is our soul's evolution.
That is why we are here. Every thought creates an energy field,
and we are energy fields, spirits, formed by the thoughts of God
– or the Godhead, as spirit-communicators refer to this force. In
the beginning we are spirit-sparks – seeds is a good way of
understanding it. We are only potential, the spiritual equivalent
of newborn babies. The spirit-spark begins to gain wisdom
through existence on all the planes of life until it evolves into a
mighty being of love, knowledge and compassion. At the end
of this great journey we return to become part of the perfect
expression of all those qualities, the Godhead. Over thousands
of years this truth has been lost, and endless souls have been lost
to the seductions of the material world – the only one we have

believed existed. The Jesus parable of the Prodigal Son was a description of the way the spirit leaves the Godhead, learns lessons, and returns. Unfortunately you can get lost sometimes on this journey which is what has happened to the human race.

Our perceptions are about to undergo an unprecedented transformation as this truth is revealed. We must be like children, wipe our minds of past misconceptions, and begin again. For instance, most people don't suffer from mental and physical handicaps by chance – their souls give themselves disabled bodies on purpose, to develop a part of their character and experience. Maybe they have treated a disabled person badly in the past and need to understand what it feels like. Maybe they made someone disabled. Perhaps they need to know how to overcome suffering and frustration. Or it could be that they are here to teach others to love, as anyone who has known a mentally-handicapped person will appreciate – they do teach us love and affection. A soul in a handicapped body can be highly evolved and that handicap ceases to be when the soul leaves the body.

Cot deaths have never been explained by medical science. Some at least are connected with karmic patterns and decisions. Sometimes a soul will decide it only needs the experience of growth in the womb and birth to balance its development, and so it returns to a spirit plane as soon as this is accomplished. This would appear to us as an inexplicable cot death. It might be that a soul incarnates and then changes its mind. Again we have the same outcome. But most often the souls of cot death babies are spiritual teachers who leave the body soon after birth to present the parents with a challenge to overcome – the agony of losing a child.

Unknown to our physical brain we set ourselves targets and lessons to learn in each earth life, so we can progress spiritually. We know roughly what is coming when we incarnate, and we know adversity can be the greatest teacher.

A message from Wang said my football career was ended by arthritis to teach me how to "get up and get on with it". The principle is exactly the same. This does not mean we should ignore disabled people or those in distress and dire circumstances – quite the opposite. The compassion we show and the help we give is one of the tests that will decide the kind of future lives we will have, or even if we need to return to earth again at all.

There is no sense of retribution in karma. It is not the product of a vengeful God. Such a being does not exist. We decide all these things for ourselves. Between earth lives on a spirit plane we look back at our last physical incarnation and decide what part of our soul's development needs improvement. The process of assessing the immediate past life can be a painful one. Once removed from the confines of the physical body, we see things with a different perspective, and we are often horrified at what we have done on earth. This is where the idea of purgatory comes from. It is this self-assessment by the soul. Once this process is over, we continue our development on a spirit plane and plan another earth life that will give us the experience we require for further evolution. If that means we lose a child or have a crippled body, then that is because we have decided it should be unless the lifeplan is affected by our free will or that of others. We can learn from every experience, particularly the unpleasant ones, and once we accept that and realise that every experience is there for a reason, life becomes so much easier.

The soul, often in consultation with others, selects parents which will offer the best chance of providing the lessons it wishes to learn, and it incarnates as their child. So when your children say they didn't ask to be born, they are wrong. More than that, they chose you to be their parents and you chose them! With each new incarnation, we are given a certain pattern of energies needed to play the role we have decided upon. These energies will attract the people and the circumstances necessary for certain experiences. Most of us are not aware of what we have come to do because that knowledge would prevent the challenges being met as planned, and being aware of what we have done in the past would be too much for most to bear. There is a mechanism which makes us forget, so we are not consciously burdened by past deeds while in a physical body. There are, however, people who specialise in helping you find out about past lives and present karma, but we are only allowed to know what we need to know and no more.

We are given the gift of free will to make our own decisions about which earth lives we shall have, or if we will keep to our life-plan once we have incarnated. Our current circumstances may not be precisely the ones we planned. When we come across a pre-arranged challenge, we may take the wrong decision. We may have married the wrong person or given up on something when we could have had the determination to continue. This is how we can be diverted from our course, and if we don't achieve what we set out to achieve, or learn what we were meant to learn, we have to come back in similar circumstances and try again.

It is the same when people commit suicide to run away from problems. There are many souls locked into a cycle of living life after life in the same circumstances because they keep making the same mistakes and don't learn the lessons, but it is comforting to know that our souls, spirit guides and guardian angels are always trying to recreate the situations which will bring us back on course. Either way, we are where we are today because of our own decisions and no one else's.

I am sure many people will say, "Hold on, if we have free will to decide our earth lives, we would all make ourselves millionaires, surely?" This is to forget that we are drawn like a magnet to a greater or lesser extent to continue our evolution, though we may not appreciate that in the confines of the diver's suit we call the physical body. If we are to evolve we have to learn, and the only way to do that is to experience different situations and emotions. In the end, we all come round to that truth, and plan our earth lives accordingly. Even what we would call 'evil' people see sense eventually. They are left to play out their misguided fantasies on the lowest nonphysical plane until they ask for help to progress.

Once they ask for help it is immediately at hand, and they are advised on how best to pay back karmic debts they have accumulated. This is never done all at once. No one is put into circumstances he or she is not equipped to handle.

Souls often incarnate in groups and play many different roles in their various earth lifetimes, male and female. All the world really is a stage and we are the actors. A soul is neither male nor female, but both, as is God. It may be that the soul of a person's wife may once have been his/her husband or child or close friend. When karmic debts are built up between certain souls, they incarnate together to pay them back. It is possible that you did something to a member or members of your family in a past life, and you are here to work off that debt with love and support – or, of course, it could just as easily be the other way round, or, most often, mutual. Groups of souls also come to earth together if they have a specific job to do for the world in general.

So much can be explained by the law of karma. It affects not only individual souls, but also families, groups, sects, companies, races, nations and humanity as a whole. The human race is facing its karma now. All build up karmic debts if they harm any form of life, and this is why we have cycles of races, countries, companies, etc., rising to the top and then collapsing in bankruptcy or suffering. It may pay us to do the right thing by all life-forms from the start, for this could help us with adverse karma.

The earth is, in effect, a spiritual university. It offers the opportunity for souls to get back on the right path if they so choose. It is, in every sense, the university of life because the challenges of living in a shell of dense physical matter are the toughest of all. The upheavals awaiting us in this decade and beyond are the hardest examination we can face, but we knew what we were letting ourselves in for when we came. We must remember, too, that we don't spend long in the classroom at any one time. We live forever, and the period we inhabit the physical body is nothing compared with eternity.

The best advice in relation to reincarnation and karma is "Do unto others as you would have them do unto you". There is a similar theme in the Bible which I feel originally related to explanations by Jesus of reincarnation. But you have so much more power over people if you can persuade them that they are judged on one life before going to heaven or hell forever and that they will only go to heaven if they believe what you want them to believe for your own benefit. This was the motiviation that led many popes and other Church and political leaders to change the Bible to suit their own ends over the centuries. When you think that it has been shown again and again that the

Vatican forged many 'historical' documents to hoodwink kings and others to do what the Roman Catholic Church wanted them to do, it is the height of naivety to believe they would not also change and forge many parts of the Biblical texts for the same reasons.

I believe there has been tinkering and change all through the Bible's life, particularly at certain points such as the time of the Roman Emperor, Constantine the Great, around AD 325. It was he who turned the Christian religion into the state Church of the Roman Empire with all the horrific implications that were to follow for anyone who did not follow the creed he insisted was right. I feel it was during his reign that references to re-incarnation were taken from the Bible. With so few people able to read and so few copies of the texts around anyway, that would not have been the enormous task it might at first appear.

I know that many others feel that re-incarnation was lost from the Bible at a meeting of the Ecumenical Church Council called by the Byzantine Emperor, Justinian at Constantinople in AD 553. The story goes that this was the result of Justinian's marriage to an actress called Theodora. He was dominated by her personality, and she effectively became ruler, and a tyrannical one at that. Her enemies were slain in large numbers and she came into bitter conflict with the Church of Rome.

At this time a sect called the *Monophysites* came onto the scene. They rejected the Christian teaching on reincarnation. Theodora became a convert to the Monophysite beliefs, not least because if reincarnation and karma were a fact, she was going to have many problems to face in her future lives, until she had learned the lessons of her actions in this one. She set about obliterating all mention of these laws in the Bible, and in doing so she presumably believed that somehow they would no longer apply to her.

Pope Agapetus admonished Justinian for allowing Theodora to appoint a yes-man as Patriarch of Constantinople, and Justinian agreed to replace him with someone acceptable to Rome. The Pope died, very conveniently, soon after. Theodora wrote to his successor Pope Silverius demanding that he reappoint the yes-man as patriarch. When the Pope received her communication he said: "I know very well ·that this affair has brought an end to my life". He stuck with his principles and refused her request. She organised a campaign of lies and character-assassination that led to him being defrocked and sent into exile, where he 'died' Such was her power that she became the first Empress to appoint her own Pope. This was Virgilius, appointed in 538. She had, by then, had two Popes murdered, and appointed another.

Theodora died around 547, but Justinian was so hypnotised by her that he continued where she left off, convinced that both would be equally powerful rulers in the great beyond, if only he could rid the Bible of all reference to reincarnation and karma. In 553, Justinian convened the Ecumenical Church Council on the pretext of agreeing a minor change to the Canon Law. However he invited only six bishops, who followed the teaching of Origen on reincarnation, while there were 159 who followed the Monophysite anti-reincarnation creed. I wonder how the voting went.

Even Theodora's Pope Virgilius was outraged, and demanded equal representation. This was turned down, and the Pope refused to attend the Council. It was at this Council that Origen was condemned as a heretic, and the decision was made to remove all references to reincarnation and karma from the Bible. I don't know if all or any of this particular story is true, but I have no doubt whatsoever that explanations of how consciousness is eternal for everyone were deleted from the Bible text for reasons of personal and collective power. Over a period of time, perhaps in a process of death by a thousands cuts, truths were removed and the Church was condemned to teach an illusion from then on. No wonder its teaching is so full of contradictions! When you consider that such fundamental passages were lost, plus the many other changes and misinterpretations, it is a near-miracle that the Bible still contains so much truth.

A few references to reincarnation do survive. The most obvious one comes after the disciples ask Christ about the predictions of the Old Testament scribes, that the prophet Elias (or Elijah) would return again before the coming of the Lord:

And Jesus answered and said unto them, "Elias shall come

first and restore all things. But I say unto you that Elias is come already, and they knew him not, but have done unto him whatever they listed. Likewise shall the Son of Man suffer of them. Then the disciples understood that He spake of John the Baptist. (*Matthew*, 17, 11-13).

The soul of the Old testament prophet Elias or Elijah had reincarnated into the body of the man we know as John the Baptist. The American psychic, Edgar Cayce, read the Bible once for every year of his life. He was, therefore, deeply shocked when he awoke from a trance in 1923 to be told that he had been saying that reincarnation was a fact. He was soon to have no doubts as the evidence mounted until it was overwhelming. Others have gone through the same process from disbelief to total belief, as they see there can be no other credible explanation for what happens to us.

I met someone who already knew about four of his past lives on earth after a reading by Judy Hall, a lady in Dorset who specialises in psychic communications and astrology, which reveal both past lives and the reason for the present one. I was intrigued and wrote to her. All she needs are a picture and the date, time and place of birth. She knew nothing of substance about what had happened to me. When her tape arrived it was quite an experience. I now believed totally in reincarnation and karma, but it is still strange to hear about who your soul had been in previous lives.

First she said that from the moment she picked up my astrological chart she was aware of "tremendous psychic energy", which she felt had been sent to help her with my reading. My purposes in this life involved the "collective power of humanity" and working to bring in change. This was confirmed, she said, by the position of the planets in the astrological area of the solar system known as Aquarius. My role would be to help bring about a spiritual revolution, and I would become a "cosmic parent" to the planet and humanity. Other planetary sequences at the time of my birth had given me enormous power to get things done and to stand up for what I believed. "I would imagine if you put your mind to doing something, nothing on Earth will shift you. You will go on when others give up, and you get there in the end. If you harness your mind with that will-for-change you can literally do anything."

There was a deep karmic purpose behind my childhood, my parents and all my relationships. In other words they were, or are, all linked to the reason I am on Earth this time. She said my purpose was to go out into the public eye and be seen to stand up for what I believed in, and to convey a new under-standing. "You have taken on quite a task – nurturing the world mentally and physically". I did, however, have plenty of help. "Psychically, I think you are surrounded – there's this huge host who are there ready and willing to help. Your task is what is important".

The whole astrological chart, Judy Hall noted, was "pretty powerful in terms of where you have been and where you are going". I had the potential to be 'incredibly psychic' with the ability to channel information down to earth from elsewhere. This power would soon be activated, and when that happened I would be put on a different plane altogether. Betty Shine had told me something similar two months earlier.

Judy said she was being told psychically that I had lived many simple lives worshipping 'the Great Mother', and gaining attunement with the cycles of the earth. These were very primi-tive lives from today's perspective, but nevertheless important because "you have total unity, total attunement. I have a sense that for the task you have, you need to go right back to your roots, really getting in touch with the earth's energy and using it to ground you so you can take off spiritually".

She then came up with three of my soul's specific past lives: the soldier, the spy and the medium. My determination to end environmental destruction had been implanted in my eternal spirit-soul after experiencing the Russian scorched-earth policy, when they burned the entire landscape to stop the advance of Napoleon. I had been a general in his army. Seeing the desola-tion had made me determined to stop environmental degrada-tion, and in that same life I had learned the futility of war, and when to retreat and re-group for another day.

She said that in the early part of this century I had lived in the south of the United States and I had been a victim of the witch-hunts against fraudulent mediums, in which the escapologist Houdini was heavily involved. I had been branded a fraud when I was not, and to have my integrity questioned and the whole meaning of my life brought into doubt had devastated me. She believed that this life had ended in suicide when I was still quite young.

She then had a vision of a spider sitting in the centre of a web and everything being brought to him. This was symbolic of many things including a life I had in the reign of Elizabeth I. I had been like that spider, at the centre of a sort of secret service, gathering intelligence. It had not been merely political information. I had received a lot of occult and esoteric knowledge which I processed and passed on to people. It had been a position of considerable power. If I had given information about people to certain quarters they would have been killed.

But apparently I didn't do that. "It's quite interesting," Judy remarked on the tape, "You had an ethical and moral stand for the work you did, when most people would regard the work as unethical". If the people in question were politicians I supported I would quietly compile a dossier on them; and if I didn't support them I would tell them I knew what they were doing and that they should desist. She said that many of those people were around me, or would be around me, in this life to pay back that debt in the form of support. They weren't forced to do this because they had free will, but their souls were giving themselves the opportunity. Another interesting aspect was that she said I'd had a strong connection with Francis Bacon, the famous philosopher, and one of the most brilliant men the world has seen. This was important because I was close enough to be aware of the knowledge he acquired.

Judy finished the tape with a look at the future. She saw a vision of an unmistakable woman from Colombia. A meeting with her was planned for me. "She's enormous, absolutely huge, with very long, dark hair. It's more or less straight, just a bit curly at the ends. She's got one of those necks that disappear into her chin, and very distinctive sloping shoulders. She is incredibly powerful, and something she says is the key to the final work you have to do. What you are about to embark on is an interim stage, and later you will be used much more as yourself. I sense that you are being used as a mouthpiece and that later your own powers will be used. This woman is to do with that. It's such a turning-point. After that I can only see you bathed in tremendous light."

Two of those past lives were difficult to follow up, but the Elizabethan one looked promising. Surely it wouldn't be hard to track down someone very close to Francis Bacon, who ran a secret service operation? It wasn't. In my local library I found a book within a few minutes called *Elizabeth and Essex*. In it were many references to a man who setup a network of information-gathering for Lord Essex, and had people all over Europe working for him. His name... Anthony Bacon, brother of Francis. It is weird in the extreme to sit there looking at a picture of someone your soul was part of 400 years ago.

In the end, Queen Elizabeth and Lord Essex fell out in rather a big way, and Anthony Bacon was a victim of that. The book summed up his last days: "Anthony Bacon found rest which this world had never given him. The terrible concatenation of events – the loss of his master, his brother, the ruin of his hopes, the triumph of folly, passion and wickedness – had broken the last prop of his shattered health, his fierce indomitable spirit." It may sound a pretty depressing end, but my soul would have learned much from those experiences, and that, after all, is the point.

A later reading with Judy revealed some of the previous links with my family in past lives. We have been together in many different roles and different countries. Kerry had been with me when I was Anthony Bacon, and we were children together in Victorian times. There was a strong link between Linda and Gareth. He had been a Tibetan monk in the incarnation before this one. Linda and I have been together so often "we could be here all day listing them all", Judy said. We had been man and wife in ancient Greece, when we had undergone a mystical marriage. This, apparently, was when our souls pledged themselves to each other for a long period into the future. It involved ceremonies lasting many days in the temple, and Judy saw a vision of us sitting on a bed of flowers in a cave above Delphi.

Linda had always seen her role in life as supporting me in my work. The tape made clear it was much more important than that. She had come to earth with a special task, as had Kerry and Gareth, and she would embark on that around 1995 or 1996. I had many links with my father, and the whole family was connected through past-life experiences. What struck me most about the tape was the way Judy had summed up the background and personalities of everyone so brilliantly, when she knew little or nothing about them, except for myself.

I went to see her at her cottage in Dorset. We talked of matters spiritual before we tried to ease some of those past lives from the memory of the soul through to the conscious brain. What happened to us in previous incarnations can affect our health and attitudes in this one, and going back to them through various techniques can lay the ghost to rest, and the health and emotional problems related to a past life disappear.

In the spiritual world beyond our sight, every thought and deed of every life-form is recorded on a fine substance known at the Akashic Records. All of us, our eternal spirit-souls that is, have our own unique vibrations, our spiritual fingerprints, and they are the means of recording what we do. This is what the Bible means when it talks of the Book of Life being opened on Judgment Day. The Akashic Records are this Book of Life. Past life memories are also held by the soul.

Our personal earth-life vibration is, it would appear, imprinted upon us at birth. What form it takes is decided by the positions of the planets at the moment we are born – a moment we have chosen. Throughout our lives we are affected by the way our vibrations relate to those created by the planetary movements, and so you have astrology. Souls are trying very hard to be born at a certain time to receive a vibration suitable for the life they wish to lead. The timing is no accident.

Judy Hall has a method which puts you into very deep meditation, although you are fully conscious and can stop at any time. The meditation is so deep that you can actually 'tune in' to your Akashic Record or soul-memories, and it will release details of past lives, all of which are stored there. But as I have said, you are only allowed the knowledge you need for your development at that time.

I wasn't given any awareness of the past when I was with Judy. Instead I had a pain in my abdomen which came and went all the way through. It was like a knife going in. At the start I felt the 'spider's web' across my face again, with the sensation along my hairline of the web being pressed down. I lost all sense of time. I thought it was about an hour I was lying there – it was more than three. It was quite unlike anything I had experienced before. What I'll never forget, though, were my hands. They first turned so cold that I lost feeling in them. Then they began to burn, almost to the point of being unbearable. Judy sat there observing me, and she had seen through her psychic vision that my body-energies, the aura that surrounds the physical body, were being rearranged. Several times during those three hours she had a vision of evolved beings having a discussion. It was a sort of Star Trek scene: they all had tiny waists and wore the same uniform. Rank was denoted by the shape of the hairstyle. I know it is hard to believe after the way we have been conditioned, but there we are – I can only tell you what happened. To disbelieve is not to disprove, as they say.

The story had hardly begun, and yet my life and percep-tions were already changing dramatically. I knew that for some reason I had a job to do in this lifetime that would, in conjunc-tion with other events and other people, change the world forever. I felt a bit isolated and lonely with the knowledge I had been given, but the Grand Plan was soon to take care of that.

It was time, as Wang said, to hold hands.

3

Letters from the Gods

The events of the next few weeks were to reveal much about the nature of the problem facing the Earth and, by definition, the whole of humanity. I was also to realise why the geological upheavals were necessary.

It relates to the Earth's energy-system. Conventional science does not accept that this even exists, but science is mistaken. I was led to a book about these energies, and once I had the basic knowledge, I was subsequently guided to many psychics who were receiving messages about this energy-system. The energy flows from a central source – the Godhead – and throughout the universe on a giant interconnecting grid that links up every planet and star. Each planet is a pulse-point that sends the energy on to the next one and so on. The stars do the same. The energy is referred to in the Bible and all the psychic communications as the Holy Spirit, the Christ Spirit or, most often, the Light.

This energy, the life-force of Creation, is carried across the Earth on what some people call *ley lines*. The ancients rightly believed that these lines were the Earth's life-blood, and made the land fertile. They are often marked by old tracks walked by people for thousands of years, though these have disappeared rapidly under new roads and developments. Birds use these lines to guide them when they migrate, and all animals are tuned into them. Every country has a version of ley lines. The ancient Chinese knew them as dragon lines, and to this day people have called geomancers, whose task it is to make the energy flow as efficiently as possible. Many energy-lines are set out with perfect symmetry, according to the laws of geometry and numerology. Pyramids and domes were built because their shapes interact with the energy. The Great Pyramid at Giza is a key point in the whole system.

I realised that ancient ceremonies and stone circles were not designed to worship false gods. The circles are power points that boosted and distributed the energy across the land, and the ceremonies involved walking, dancing and singing, in a way that stimulated the energy and charged it up. In 1921, a man called Alfred Watkins was enjoying the view from the top of a hill in Herefordshire when suddenly he saw before his eyes, not the landscape of the 1920s but that of ancient England. He could see a network of lines linking all the old stones, crosses, moats, holy wells, special trees with legends attached, and churches on pre-Christian sites. These were all in direct alignment with each other, and they linked up in the same fashion with beacon hills and mountain tops. After this vision, he began to investigate ley-lines, and found they matched up perfectly with what he had seen. He published his findings in a book, *The Old Straight Track*. Energy-lines, however, do not necessarily have to be straight. They can be created anywhere that people or animals walk regularly, because we are all made up of energy fields, and so we can form energy-lines if we walk the same way often enough. They can also be created by thought.

The messages coming through from many sources explained how this energy-system was in urgent need of restoration. If it wasn't restored, the earth would die, and the universe would suffer a catastrophe as the energy-grid was broken. When people walked everywhere and made pilgrimages down the long-distance paths, as in *Pilgrim's Progress,* the movement stimulated the energy. In doing so the walkers charged themselves with the life-force. Now we use cars and are covering more of the earth with concrete and tarmac, and this interchange between people, earth and energy cannot take place as it should. More than that, cars, electricity pylons, broadcasting transmitters and other things are causing great damage to the natural energy-lines which have survived.

The spirit realms, and beings from other planets and star systems are now trying to restore the flow of energy before it is too late. They are working with humans in every country to patch up the old energy-grid around the Earth and build a new one ready for the more powerful energies that are being beamed to the planet. When the moment is right the energy will be switched from one system to the other. The major problem has been the destructive thoughts for which humanity has become famous throughout the universe. I mean the thoughts of hatred, anger, fear, aggression, sadness, resentment, depression, and so on. I will use the words *dark* or *darkness* to describe these thoughts and the energy they create. Some people call them *negative*, but this has several meanings, not all of them bad, and can cause confusion. Anyway, darkness sums up their effect and contrasts them clearly with the Light.

The Earth's energy-system can be blocked or diminished by dark emotions and events. All our thoughts create energy-fields, and the vibrations caused by bloodshed, battles and suffering in all its forms can produce a sort of screen through which the Earth's energy cannot pass – at least not in the way it should. When you consider the thoughts of anger, fear, hatred and resentment which have been produced over the centuries, it is not hard to understand why the energy-system is in such disarray.

The Earth is a living, breathing, spiritual being, and her sadness at the damage and destruction caused by human activity has also produced much dark energy. This has blocked many of the energy-lines within the Earth and has created enormous dangers. Some areas of the planet are not absorbing enough of the life-force, and they are dying; while inside the Earth, energy is building up as its means of escape is closed off by shields of darkness. The Earth would simply explode if this situation was left unchecked, and relieving this pressure is one reason why the earthquakes and volcanoes must come.

Spirit messages made it obvious even at this stage that

ancient knowledge about energy and reincarnation and karma have been carried by certain souls through the centuries, in peoples and movements such as the early Christians, the Chaldeans, Gnostics, Cathars and Druids, and the Essenes, authors of the Dead Sea Scrolls. Jesus of Nazareth studied with the Essenes during some of the 'lost' years in the Gospels, before he was baptised by John the Baptist and began the work the Bible describes.

Old Druid sites often came up in these early months of my tutelage. The Druids were the priestly, learned class of the Celts, a people of ancient Europe who came to Britain around 500 BC. They too believed in reincarnation and were guardians of the energy-system. The Druidic religion diminished under the Romans, and all but disappeared by AD 500. Many of the souls which carried the ancient knowledge through the centuries have apparently reincarnated in our generation to play a part in bringing back the old wisdom, and to ease the transition to the new tomorrow.

This information began to emerge after I met someone living at Kenilworth in Warwickshire. I had been asked to speak at the opening of a Green Show at the National Exhibition Centre near Birmingham, and I took the chance to visit the stand of *Kindred Spirit*, a magazine for people interested in mystical and spiritual matters. The conversation turned to earthquakes, and I was told that a woman who was getting spirit communications about earthquakes had visited the stand, and was wondering what to do with these messages. It turned out that the woman had not, at that stage, received any messages about earthquakes – she had received her first message on the day of an earthquake. But that misunderstanding was essential to grab my attention. The woman had left her address with *Kindred Spirit*, and I went to see her. It was clear within a few minutes that we were meant to meet.

She was receiving what mediums call *automatic* writing. This is when a spirit sends thought forms into the subconscious, and these are processed by the physical brain to produce written words. I will refer to the woman only as 'the source'. She was one of a growing number of people that were being contacted with messages relevant to this book and The Plan in general. On the day of the British earthquake she was sitting at the type-writer in her study when she felt a tremendous push in the back. Her heavy wooden chair tipped forward and she was, as she put it, "catapulted onto the keyboard". It was as if someone had grabbed the chair and pushed it from behind. She stood up and called out but there was only silence. She checked the rest of the house and found no one. What was most strange was an over-whelming feeling that she was being urged to do something. She had experienced some psychic phenomena in the past and had heard of automatic writing. As the incident involved a typewriter, maybe she was being asked to write something. She decided to sit at the desk and write whatever came into her mind. The first sentence was already forming and after that another word came, then another. Slowly the words built up, and this is what they said:

> Only good will come from the written word that I write here. The spirit of trees and the green earth surrounds me. On the plain a single tree tells a story I can't quite remember. The sound of men and horses survive in the echo of the past. All these voices are there to be heard. They come in silence filling the valley with the strength of their numbers. There has been bloodshed. Also the mystery of words kept inside great books in the care of hooded men. The words are to be unravelled, the story told. There is fear of destruction, a secret somewhere which holds together this place. Here there was quiet, now it is trampled upon.

> Somewhere there is a Light that must continue to shine. Destruction, destruction. Hold fast to the truth that walks the way, follow the paths that lead to the hills, wash in the water over the stones. Turn them until the sound is made. There will be power to guide the feet along the tracks, beacons make a line. They will end in high places, for it is the looking down on Creation that will preserve all things. I am the Way, the Truth and the Light. Follow that Light, touch as you pass. Look to the ripples, they must be counted. There the feet have made marks and the energy lives. It can be stroked. Look into the Sun with closed eyes. Let the tree branches

carry the Light in different directions. This is the old way in the hills. The rocks remember where the fires burned. The men must walk if it is to be saved. Follow the paths. The energy must flow again. Take care. Carry the rock.

She didn't understand these words, nor where they came from, but Diane, a psychic friend, said she had been to a meeting a few days earlier at which a man had talked about ley-lines and earth energies. She thought the writing could be connected with these. It was. The source contacted the man and they arranged to meet. He arrived with a friend called John; both men are extremely psychic. The three of them agreed that at least part of the message was about energy-lines blocked in Kenilworth, which had long been an important energy site. This was recognised by Queen Elizabeth I, who was told of the energysystem by her Celtic predecessors, the Tudors, and a series of sluices and waterways were built at Kenilworth Castle. This is significant because water carries the energy.

John said Kenilworth was on a main energy-line through England, and psychic messages revealed that the energy was blocked at a point just downstream from the castle. This was where the bodies had been heaped after a battle in the 13th century, and the dark energy thus produced had caused the blockage. They visualised the energy flowing again through that area and the line was cleared.

It may sound strange that you can do this without even visiting the site, but the energy-fields created by thought can travel anywhere instantly. This is how telepathy works. Good thoughts will always disperse dark ones if they are projected strongly enough, and in this way the screens of darkness can be broken. I should stress, however, that not every block can be erased from afar. Some sites must be walked or visited by people gifted with certain energies or energy-patterns.

More automatic writing followed. A group of people were gathered together by the source and the messages sent them off to many places around the Heart of England. They were led to stone circles and ley-lines which had to be cleared. The locations were not normally mentioned by name, but only described. There were many remarkable incidents. One message had said:

"On the hill-top I will wait where the dancers (a stone circle) move, and look back over the valley to see the signs that I have marked for you". When they arrived at that spot on a dull, dark day with no sign of the sun, a shaft of sunlight pierced the cloud cover and illuminated a church down in the valley. The church, it transpired, marked the point on a ley-line where the energy was not flowing correctly. Another time the source went to a place which the writing called the Moon Grove, a Druid site. We know it by another name. She found at least eight blackbird feathers speared into the ground so firmly she struggled to pull them out. The message had said: "The feathers will become spears".

The most memorable event for the Kenilworth Group came at the Moon Grove. The message had said:

> Come again to the Moon Grove and begin the work we have shown. Wait until the Moon is full and you have seven people, and the words will come. Listen to my voice as the sun sets and the moon begins her journey across the sky. The ash tree stands sentinel, and the water must run over your feet before you begin. Say the prayers that are in your hearts, and the pendulum will show you the place where you must worship the Sun and the Moon Goddess. The oak leaves are to be held as I have told you before. They hold the memories of Albion and cannot be forgotten.

The Druids held the oak tree to be sacred, and Albion is an ancient name for England. The pendulum refers to dowsing: this is when you hold a pendulum, and it responds to questions by swinging one way or the other, to indicate *yes* or *no*. It can identify energy-lines, and the more it swings the more powerful the energy. The pendulum is also a means for the spirit world to communicate on a *yes* or *no* basis. It has many uses, but accuracy can vary greatly depending on the skill or psychic ability of the person involved. I had been taught how to dowse a few months before this all started, by a friend who used the pendulum for diagnosis in his alternative healing practice.

The source had no problems getting together the seven people required by the message. "They just sort of arrived", she

said. There was herself, her friend Diane, their husbands, two
friends, Michael and Helen, plus Deborah Shaw, who had just
returned from Canada for a short stay in Kenilworth, where she
had once lived. She had begun to have regular psychic experiences, and her place in the group was confirmed when she said
that every time she opened one of her books it fell open at a page
about a stone circle which the group had been working on. I had
a specific message from the source that I had to meet Deborah
Shaw, and we were to work closely together a few months later
when she was back in Canada.

The seven who went to the Moon Grove appeared to be
linked by past lives in ancient Sumer – between the rivers Tigris
and Euphrates in what is modern-day Iraq. They had all been
either Chaldeans or Akkadians – or at least the communications
pointed that way.

At the Moon Grove there is a pool and a stream. The
source walked through the stream as instructed, and stood on a
stone by a thorn tree. She had an oak twig in each hand. The
other six stood on the opposite side of the stream and waited for
the moment to arrive. The sun set at 8.36pm, and the moon rose
at 8.40. At 8.36pm precisely one great ripple spread itself across
the pool. The water had previously been perfectly still.

The night before, the source had spoken to a psychic
friend, and he had picked up the words she had to say: "Solache,
maker and bender of light, hear my words. Bend my golden
light into trust (or truth, it wasn't clear), redeeming one". She
repeated these words as she stood on the stone. She held up the
oak branches, as an earlier message had instructed, and she felt a
powerful force drop through her from head to foot. As this
happened her eyelids were pushed down. Her body had been
used to convert energy from above into a form the Earth could
absorb. It came in through the top of her head and out through
her feet, via her own energy pattern.

As she opened her eyes another big ripple swept across the
water. They all could also hear the sound of fish breaking the
surface of the water in the gathering darkness. The other six
now felt they should walk to the top of the hill, and there they
found hundreds of sheep walking towards them in almost regi-
mented rows. The sheep made no sound, not one *baa-a*. Part of

the Moon Grove message had said: "The beasts will acknow-ledge you in silence". As the Moon came up every single sheep turned to look intently in its direction.

When the six returned to the pool, they found the water, once so still, bubbling and gurgling out into the stream. Mas-sive ripples swept across the pool as fish leapt out of the water. All was a cascade of movement, sound, and life. It was an amazing sight and astonished those in the group who had been sceptical. In the car home, two of the number said they'd heard singing or chanting in the same spot at the Grove, and Diane said she'd had a vision of men in hooded white cloaks at the same place. The communications had spoken of "the mystery of words kept inside great books in the care of hooded men ... Men in white cloaks who have carried the knowledge ...and sing the song you have heard since the youth time." This 'youth time' referred to young souls, not children in this life. My message from Wang Yee Lee, which said: "He was chosen as a youngster for his courage" had the same meaning. This plan for the great changes on Earth was arranged, and the personnel selected, many thousands of years ago. The meaning of 'sing the songs' will become clear soon.

The event at the Moon Grove is only one of countless incidents all over the world as Operation-Change-the-Earth enters its final stages. The author of the Kenilworth Letters, a being called Ashad, spoke often of following the sun to other time zones, where others heard his words. One communication said: "There are others who hear our commands and are ready for the time when they must speak (for instance, when this book is published). Together you will be a mighty army, and you must speak with a loud voice for all the nations of the world to hear."

I was also being mentioned in some of the writing – as with "The man must write the book and all will then be known", and, "The man who writes the book will begin it all", but what was most interesting to me was the confirmation of the mes-sages I was getting from elsewhere. The rivers they speak of are the ley-lines, and the water-channels which carry energy across and through the Earth:

The world is changing, and the North will become South and the East, West. So it has been commanded since the beginning of all time. It will happen as the leaves fall from the trees and the water winds through the valley. We shall be replaced by the new gods (as one age is replaced by another), but our time has not yet come and all must be left undisturbed for the new masters.

There is much to be done and I must speak through you to the people who know of the Word. There is a darkness that will come in a lifetime and will spread over all things. The Light will be dimmed, but you have the power to preserve the fruits of the Earth. There is a blight across the land, and the Earth is dying without the prayers. You are the people of the memory who know of the old ways... there are so few left, and the work must be done. In the beginning we knew the shape of things to come, but much has been changed, and man has worked his magic in the wrong way.

The old ways are reviled, and men with forked tongues seek only wealth and have no thought for the generations that are to come. We must protect their right, and the sword (the new, more powerful energies) must flash again across our kingdom... The sword shall enter in the kingdom of the Brigantes (an ancient tribe which once controlled most of Northern England).

We shall come in the thunder, and the wind shall blow across the land. The sea will rise and there is much to be cleansed. All men must turn again to their true gods. Each knows his line and the names he must worship if the world is to be saved.

There are false gods in the land, and men with loud voices listen not to the words of their fathers. They are no longer listening to the seasons, but must try to change all things themselves. We are the gods and it is not for man to accomplish our work. Know that we must take command and put right those things that have been misarranged.

There have been many prophets, but the warnings have gone unheeded. We speak, and the land becomes silent waiting for the work to begin, but the men must move from the water for the land will be covered by the sea, and it must flow up the valleys. Many will be lost if they do not heed our warnings.

Men have not understood what is the nature of life on Earth. Much has been forgotten, and wisdom has taken the wrong path. You must return to the knowledge of your forefathers, or there will be a rent in the universe and the Light will go out. Know that we mean only kindness to all men, and as before we come only when the need is very great. There are still good things to be found on Earth and many good words spoken. But from many mouths there is only anger and bitterness and dissatisfaction at the life that was provided.

The Earth, has become weak under the burden placed upon her and the power must flow again. Everything has been planned and will come to pass as we say. For our task has been to preserve the Earth from its centre where the fire lives. The universe needs the life the Earth brings forth, and the Whole must be preserved. It is not for you alone that we do this work. There has always been an order in the way the planets have been governed. Man has not understood the linkages which bind everything together.

A much later communication went into more detail about what happens in the centre of the Earth:

The fire which is at the very heart of your world needs to be replenished after periods of time. This is because the energy it transmutes, and which holds all life together, can only reproduce itself for a certain period. The rocks, which are at the Earth's core, spread in different directions and are layered in such a way that the heat can continuously smoulder without spreading outward and crumbling the Earth from the inside.

At this time, many changes are occurring in the Earth's core and the volcanoes will soon erupt as the pressure becomes unsafe within the surface. You should look to the East for the first signs. The earthquake cycle has begun and many will be triggered by the movement that has already occurred.

The words could hardly have been clearer. The Earth faced a period of enormous change, and if this 'cleansing' did not happen the universe would suffer a catastrophe of its own. This was no dream or illusion I was involved in here. This was for real.

One thing that was apparent almost from the start was the importance of sound. This was emphasised when the Kenilworth source was led to a book called the *Shrine of Wisdom* which fell into her hands in a shop selling old books. It was a collection of journals of the same name published in the 1920s. The journals were, said the book, "A quarterly devoted to synthetic philosophy, religion, and mysticism". There was a section about special words carried through the ages by members of the ancient cultures, including the Celts, Greeks, Egyptians, Chinese, Sumerians and Chaldeans. All these words begin with 'A', and the sound they make stimulates, tunes up, one chord or frequency of the energy. The words have to be spoken with the hands across the nose and mouth; this forms a chamber in which the sound can resonate.

What is produced by some words is not unlike the sounds made by Aborigines in Australia. You put your hands together in front of you in the classic saying-your-prayers position and then bring them back to cover your face, covering your nose and mouth with your thumbs on your cheeks. "It has been too long since the prayers have been spoken", and these were the prayers it was talking about. It was the same with "Sing the songs you have sung since the youth time". Everyone involved in The Plan knew of this sound system of words when our souls lived in the ancient civilisations, and the words we used then have been given to us to say again today, to tune up the energy. Another piece of automatic writing said: "Play on the strings with your words and the Light will be enhanced". The other kind of prayers, by the way, the kind we say in church, are powerful thought-forms which are picked up by the spirit realms and acted upon or otherwise on their merit.

Much can be explained by the use and effects of sound which, if projected to the right frequency, can manifest and de-manifest rocks, cause things to levitate, and make apparently impregnable structures crumble. The age-old questions of how Stonehenge or the pyramids were built and what made the walls of Jericho come tumbling down, can now be potentially answered – the use of sound. Humanity has forgotten this wisdom to its cost.

Many strange and wonderful things were happening to me as I was led from place to place gathering knowledge. I went with the Kenilworth source to a stone circle to have my own energy charged up, and we arranged to meet her psychic friend, Diane, at a hotel nearby. After an hour she still hadn't turned up and we had to leave. The following day the source rang to say she had solved the mystery of the missing Diane. There had been a psychic message to say I shouldn't meet her yet. Diane had been in the hotel lounge in the right place at exactly the same time we were there and we walked the length of the lounge on several occasions in the course of that hour. But Diane had not seen us and we had not seen her.

Another time I was on holiday in Venice when I visited an island called Burano, which is famous for its lace-making. I wandered into the church of San Martino and stood looking up at a large painting of Christ. As I looked, the picture turned black and moved around before my eyes. Only the face of Christ was still. Suddenly I felt a sensation I can only describe as someone pushing a pneumatic drill into the top of my head. I gripped the pew I was standing beside and my body vibrated from the top of my head to the base of my spine as something seemed to go through me. It lasted for maybe half a minute, and when it stopped my eyes focused again and the painting went back to normal. Months later I was told that this had been the moment I received a gift of energy from one of the Masters of this planetary system. The energy was to give me strength and courage, a determination to seek the truth, and the confidence that I would find it.

We were all getting tremendous help and support from the spirit beings who were controlling and co-ordinating The Plan. Whatever we did, they had an expert in that field to offer expertise and guidance. This book is an example of that. At another visit to Betty Shine, a message told me to start writing and the information would be given to me: "They're giving me the name of the man who will be working with you", Betty said. "Paul... Paul, no, I can't get it... they'll give it to me again in a minute." A short silence followed. "Paul Branston, no, Branton... that's his name, Paul Branton – they say you will not have heard of him, but he is very spiritual and a wonderful writer. He will help you shape the book". She added: "They are telling me to go to my bookcase and I will find a book he has written. Well, that's a load of rubbish for a start!"

Betty was moving to another house, and only a few books she had never got around to reading remained at this one. She left the room, certain the information was wrong. "You will never believe it", she said as she returned. "I bought this book with five others a year ago, and I've never read it. I forgot I had it." She held up the book: *The Quest – Vol II, The Notebooks of Paul Brunton.* He was an American who wrote widely on spiritual matters before his death in 1981. Betty also told me it would be better if I left the Isle of Wight before the winter because I would soon be travelling almost constantly, and living on an island would make my travel arrangements more difficult and complicated. I couldn't move that quickly, but her words proved to be perfectly correct.

My many journeys toward enlightenment were soon to begin.

4

The Grand Design

Learning more than I ever had before about the true nature of life was a wondrous and humbling experience. The universe is one big brotherhood and sisterhood of souls. There is no division. All is one and one is all.

Over the months I was able to piece together the basic structure within which we all live. This was done either by direct communications or by reading books or parts of books, which were subsequently confirmed as basically accurate by direct communications.

Every form of life is created by the same light-energy, whatever we may be. We are governed by the same laws, and so we conform to the same basic spiritual design, albeit with differences in detail. Every form, including the Godhead, has two opposite poles, positive-negative or male-female, whichever you prefer to call them. We are all searching for the perfect balance between these forces, and when we find this harmony we are at one with the Creator. We are home again.

What we call *evil* is the manifestation of a soul considerably out of balance – evil is disharmony of the soul. Hell is not a place, but a state of mind. Both poles are necessary to find the perfection of balance which leads us to what the Bible calls heaven. Again, heaven is not a place, but a state of mind, a state of being.

It is by experiencing too much negative and too much positive that we find the point of balance between them. *Evil* is when this experience is taken to extremes. All of creation is constantly seeking the neutral point between conflicting forces. In the modern world the masculine polarity has been dominant at the expense of the caring, compassionate, receptive, feminine. It has been grab-and-take rather than help-and-give. The next age will seek to redress that imbalance. Male and female polarities, I should point out, are within us all, it is not a man-woman division.

It is a cosmic law that when two forces, male-female, positive-negative, unite, a third force is created. This could be where the concept of the religious Trinity originates, the Father-Mother-Son or, in Western religions where the feminine has been discarded, the Father-Son-Holy Spirit. It is the interplay between the positive and negative poles of each entity that keeps energy vibrating at a particular rhythm and sets one vibration apart from another. The closer the two poles are to harmony the quicker the vibration, and this is how we progress up the ladder of frequencies to the Godhead. The only difference between lifeforms or objects in terms of how they appear is the speed at which the energy is vibrating and their level of evolution. We may see a 'solid' shape, but in fact it is not solid. Nothing is. Our own science has acknowledged that what we think is solid is really energy vibrating at a certain speed. The slower it vibrates, the denser the form appears. The faster it vibrates, the more transparent it looks, until the vibrations are too quick for our physical eyes to see.

Radio waves are invisible to us for this very reason. This is also why there are so many reports of people seeing UFOs which suddenly 'disappear'. What the UFOs have done is switch frequencies from one we can see to one we cannot. Energy and physical matter are the same substance. Matter is energy vibrating slowly, and when matter is burned or decays the process quickens the vibrations and it breaks down into pure energy again. It really is true to talk of the rhythm of life: that is an excellent description of these principles.

There is One Consciousness in Creation and we are all aspects of that Consciousness. I have described us as like droplets of water in an ocean, all part of the same whole. This whole, however, is not all at the same level of evolution and development. This One Consciousness is made up of endless levels of awareness and understanding. These are the frequencies of life I talk about. They are frequencies of consciousness. At the highest level, what I call the Godhead or the Ultimate, is the sum total of Creation's wisdom, love, and understanding. The further down the frequencies you go, the further you are away from that state-of-the-art consciousness.

These frequencies of life are not stacked on top of each other like a chest of drawers, they share the same space. Wherever you are reading this book will contain in the space you are occupying all the frequencies in Creation, including the Ultimate or Godhead.

We can't see these other levels because they are vibrating at a speed beyond the range our eyes and physically-attuned brains can tune into, although mediums and sensitives can quicken their own rate of vibration enough to contact other dimensions or 'frequencies'. This is why they see or hear spirits and others do not. It is also possible for souls on other planes to lower their vibrations enough to be seen as a transparent outline, sometimes more, in our physical world. On these occasions we see them as ghosts. They can walk through walls because there is a vast difference between their frequency and that of the wall, just as radio waves can pass through our houses to reach the transistor. On their own level these souls look perfectly solid to each other because they are operating within the same frequency range.

Each higher plane and sub-plane of frequency is more wonderful than the one below as we get closer and closer to the perfect balance of peace, love, will, knowledge and wisdom that is our ultimate destiny. The astral plane is the nearest to the physical, and a communication from a consciousness called Attarro, of whom much more later, gave us some idea of what life is like there:

I want to tell you of the beauty of the astral levels. The beauty is beyond explanation. The cleanliness of our air is refreshing and crystal clear. The greenness of our trees is of hues humans could not yet distinguish. We visit churches of resounding reverence, walk in marble streets of harmony wherever we step. The learning process is everlasting. We meet and exchange our knowledge from all existences to gain perspective on God's plan. Earth, so far away (in frequency), yet so near, is rocking the balance, not only of the cosmos, but of the astral plane, and we seek to gain balance and harmonise your world.

It is to the astral plane I was told that we go when the physical body dies. Depending on our spiritual evolution, we either stay there until our next earth life or move through to a higher plane. People who have died and been brought back to life recall seeing a light at the end of a tunnel at the point of death. As they reach the light they see an exquisite place of incredible beauty and amazing colours where they meet 'dead' friends and relatives. What they have done is visit the astral plane before returning to the physical body. The only difference between that and death is that when we die we stay there. The consciousness of people in a coma moves to the astral plane while they decide if they wish to continue their physical life or stay where they are. If they decide to come back they emerge from the coma, if they decide not to come back they 'die'.

On the astral and all levels of life, other than the physical, we take our nourishment from the energy around us, and everything else we need we produce by thought. You think it and it appears before you. This applies also to your appearance. You look how you need to look. To think, we wear black and go through agonies when our loved ones die, and yet all they have done is move on to a place of breathtaking magnificence where we will eventually join them! We are not that far from the day when funerals will be joyous affairs, a celebration that a soul has completed a set of lessons and has returned to the nonphysical world.

Another fundamental difference between the physical and non-physical planes is time. They have no such thing as time in the way we measure it. Only on earth are we obsessed with the clock and make such a great distinction between past, present and future. On the spirit-planes all three are happening at once and they come together in the Now. This is a state of being which is virtually impossible for our physical brains to comprehend at this stage of our evolution, and I mention it only in passing. Incidentally, this difference in the concept of time makes it very difficult for spiritual guides to tell us precisely when events will occur, and you should keep this in mind, when I mention specific dates.

The human being incarnated on earth has a constant link with the astral, mental, spiritual and soul planes. Part of us permanently exists there during an earth life. The human entity is made up of many bodies, not just the physical one we see. First there is the real us, the spirit-soul. This takes on a spiritual body, a mental body, or mind, and an astral or emotional body, which, obviously, is the source of the person's emotional responses. The more evolved the soul, the more adeptly it will manage the emotions and personality of the person. The less evolved souls are usually dominated by their other bodies and so allow emotion and the limited perspective of the physical brain to rule them. It is all part of the learning process.

Throughout our lives on earth, while the physical body operates on the physical frequency which we can see, all the other bodies operate on their own frequencies, which we can't see. The soul can move its consciousness from one body to another and that is all that happens in physical death. Consciousness is removed from the physical body.

In fact, this happens to us when we sleep. Every night our consciousness moves to the astral body and we travel around the astral plane. We meet loved ones who have died, and the more evolved will spend time with spiritual teachers or discuss special tasks we may be involved in on earth. Most people don't remember the details of this when they awake, but these travels are one reason for our dreams. They usually appear as weird or amazing dreams. This is the physical brain trying to make sense of scenes it cannot comprehend. During these nightly travels the astral body is connected to the physical by a thin thread of energy and when we show signs of waking the astral body returns instantly. Often people will have a premonition that someone has died, because their astral bodies have met on one of these occasions.

The spirit-soul and its non-physical bodies incarnate in the womb and take on a physical shell. This shell is, itself, made up of two bodies, the one we see and another called the etheric. This organises the growth and development of the physical body. The human entity, as we have seen, is a series of bodies or energy-fields, and the etheric is the master organising-field. DNA, to which medical science has given a great deal of attention, carries the genetic code which explains to the individual cells how to do their job and what kind of cell they will be, but the etheric body holds the information about where that cell should go and what it should do on a second-by-second basis. It is the blueprint, the template, for the physical body. The etheric field is responsible for growth, the physical shape, the repair of damage and injury, recovery from illness, and so on. If you could see the etheric body around the unformed foetus, you would see it was shaped like the body it is destined to become. This applies to all things.

The health and harmony of the mental and astral or emotional bodies can either support, control, or disrupt this etheric organisation, because they are all energy fields interacting with each other. This is how our mental and emotional states can filter through to become physical illness. When modern medicine realises this, there will be a revolution in health care. We will at last judge our medical success by how few people are ill and not, as now, on how many ill people we treat. Physical illness is caused by the disruption of the etheric organisation, and this can happen weeks, months or even years before we feel physical discomfort. When we have found ways to test for this disruption and re-stabilise the etheric energy-field, physical illness will be reduced on a quite fantastic scale.

Here lies a cure for cancer and heart disease, which are caused, like so much illness, by the emotional and mental bodies affecting the etheric. This disruption can also damage the immune system, so making us open to diseases that we would normally repel quite easily. We so often see a husband or wife die, or become very ill, soon after his or her partner has died. This is caused by the shock and grief of the loss affecting the etheric organisation, or damaging the immune system. It has become known as 'dying of a broken heart'. Disease is literally what it says, dis-ease, disharmony. Of course, the mental body can also work the other way to re-balance the etheric organisation and cure illness. This is what we call mind over matter.

The etheric organisation is also prone to outside influences such as electromagnetism, and I remember reading a report which said that those working with electromagnetism are much more at risk from some sorts of cancer. This is because the etheric body is being thrown out of balance by electromagnetic influences, and a certain type of cancer is the result. You can explain so many things once you accept that the etheric body exists. When people have limbs amputated they often feel as if the limb is still there, and this happens because the etheric body is still there in the shape of the limb. In the new age, we will understand how to stimulate the etheric body so that it will regrow lost limbs, just as some animals do today. It is the pre-arranged disorganisation of the etheric body which produces difficult physical karma in an earth life. This may happen in the womb, producing a deformed or handicapped baby, or it may happen later in the form of a heart attack, cancer, or, in my case, arthritis.

The etheric body is within the overall frequency band known as the physical and can be seen by many psychics and sensitives, but it is at the higher end of the band and is still vibrating too quickly for most people to see. Many more will have this etheric sight, however, as new vibrations are tuned up. All our various bodies come together in the *aura*, which surrounds the physical body, and this provides the outer shield against unwanted energies and influences around us. Again, many sensitives can see this and diagnose illness by studying its colours.

The more spiritually-developed the soul, the bigger, more powerful, will be this energy surrounding the head and body. This is where the halo comes from in Biblical pictures. You have people depicted with a bright glow around them, or with a thin ring over the head, with which we see them depicted so often in paintings, statues and children's books.

All our bodies are also linked together by energy points called *chakras*, which are vital to our emotional and physical

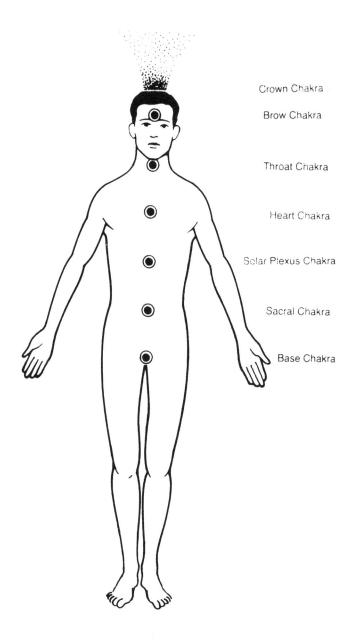

Crown Chakra

Brow Chakra

Throat Chakra

Heart Chakra

Solar Plexus Chakra

Sacral Chakra

Base Chakra

The Seven Chakras

health and wellbeing. Throughout our lives we are absorbing energy, the life-force of Creation, which is all around us. Without this we could not exist. The chakras work with this energy, and when they are operating correctly they look like spinning wheels of colour. The chakras act as booster-points for the energy (like stone circles), help to distribute the energy around the body along meridian lines (human ley-lines), and 'step down' the energy into a form the body can use. Chakras are vortices of energy which link together the levels of being.

When the chakras are working properly and the energy-system is in harmony, we are in good health. When there is a block in a meridian or chakra caused by mental or emotional imbalances, this shows itself in physical or further emotional problems. Chinese acupuncture has been based on this principle of energy-lines and power points for thousands of years. The stainless steel needles are placed at points along the meridian lines to rebalance and harmonise the energy-system. Stones sited on ley-lines are there for the same reason. There are seven main chakras on each body, though there are also other power points along every meridian line. The main chakras are at the base of the spine, the sex organs, solar plexus, heart, throat, forehead, and on top of the head – this last one is known as the crown chakra. Each chakra vibrates to the frequency of a spectrum colour. They all have their individual physical and emotional responsibilities, and all are connected to the physical body through the glands of the endocrine system. The lower chakras are concerned with everyday and earthly matters and the top three with overall matters and the spiritual. The heart chakra is the meeting point, the bridge of balance between them.

The forehead chakra is linked to the 'third eye' or all-seeing eye, a sort of spiritual telescope through which we see our psychic visions and understand life. It was a psychic projection of this eye that I could see everywhere soon after this story began. When people talk about opening your third eye, they mean activating your psychic powers, which we all have, though some more than others. The crown chakra is the point of entry for thought-forms from the spirit realms, which sensitives can turn into words. It is through this chakra that we tune into higher levels of intelligence and wisdom.

So when we stand in front of a mirror we are looking at more than our physical shape. Out of range of our eyes are the etheric body, the astral or emotional, the mental or mind, the spiritual, and the spirit-soul. Each of them is operating in its own plane of existence, while making up the physical entity for the short stay on Earth. The laws of life are this: our outer body must always be vibrating at the frequency of the plane we are working on, and we must carry within us bodies from all the other planes that separate the outer body from the soul – that is, the soul could not operate in a physical body without the astral, mental and spiritual bodies. We progress up the frequencies by quickening the vibration of the soul, and we do that by the quality of our thoughts, actions, love, wisdom and understanding. Extreme negative emotions if not balanced by positive can create an imbalance which lowers the vibratory state and causes us to fall down the frequencies of consciousness.

What I have described in relation to the human entity is the Grand Design for all forms of life, including the planet. The Earth, too, is a soul that takes on an emotional, mental, spiritual and etheric body for its incarnation into the physical body which we live on. The etheric body of the earth carries the blueprint to organise, repair, balance and harmonise the physical, in response to natural events or human activities which promote imbalance and disharmony. This etheric organisation is better known to us as the laws of nature. Some environmentalists call it *Gaia*, named after the Greek Goddess of the Earth.

The universe is based throughout on the law of *as above, so below*. Everything conforms to the same basic design, everything is a microcosm of the whole. Individual countries have a consciousness to guide them, and so do planets, solar systems, cosmic systems and so on. There is truly one grand design behind everything.

This is extremely significant for those of us on the Earth today. If the health of our own emotional and mental bodies affects the etheric blueprint, and eventually shows itself in physical disease, then exactly the same happens to the Earth. If her mental and emotional state is out of balance then her etheric organisation will be disrupted, and physical manifestations of this will occur. So much of the environmental mayhem we see in the world is the result of the Earth-spirits' emotional and mental turmoil caused by human activity, and I understand that one of my main jobs, apart from writing books, is to try, with others, to stabilise and strengthen the earth's emotional and mental state. If she is upset then we take the consequences, and I know that after the way humanity has treated her for so long she is currently having serious mental and emotional problems. She needs our help – and fast.

5

Spirit of the Stones

I was sent on many travels around England and Wales clearing energy-blockages, charging up energy-centres, and learning about the powers of the mineral kingdom – what most people look upon as dead rock.

I went on one trip with John, the psychic who went to see the Kenilworth source after her first communication. Our destination was Wales, where we were to meet Joan, who was also working on the energy-system. On the way to see her, we were sent by a psychic message to find two stones buried on a hillside somewhere on the England-Wales border. John dowsed the map to establish approximately where the stones were, and we parked the car at the end of a narrow road which eventually became a rough track.

It was a magical place. As we walked, the energy was quite the most powerful I had felt. Both of us were struggling to put one foot in front of the other. The pendulum led us to the top of a colossal man-made hill where the views touched your soul. The view down across the valley and away to the hills and mountains on the darkening horizon was something that will stay with me forever. The sun was turning a deepening gold with its journey over Britain almost complete for another day.

The scene was awesome, just awesome.

We dowsed to find the right spot, a pile of stones and earth left by the Celts, and after much digging and a broken spade we found the stones we were looking for. The minerals have spirits just as we do, and they can store information. They can act as a sort of spiritual computer disc. The ancient peoples transferred knowledge of the energies and the future to the spirits of the stones. It was not easy to walk away from that hilltop as night began to fall. I felt so much at peace in that place. The sun sparkled its patterns across the sky as we made our descent, and it was later to deliver the most spectacular sunset I had seen.

The following day we were sent with Joan to three other sites on the Welsh borders. The two stones we picked up the previous night were to be used at the first location. It was at the top of a hill in a field of sheep, and we were presented with another magnificent panorama across the valleys. As we had driven away from Joan's house, John realised he had left the stones on the roof of the car. We found them lying in the road. One was okay, but the other had broken in two. Yet when the instruction came through about what was to be done on the hill, we found we indeed needed three pieces of stone!

We were asked to find a fourth large stone in the field, and John picked up the only one we could see. As he did so, this big chunk of stone broke in two in his hands. The break was so clean the pieces still fitted together perfectly. The small stones had to be arranged into a triangle with the big one in the middle, and the information was passed from the spirits of the three into the one. John, who can tune to the frequency of the mineral kingdom, said it sounded like the human equivalent of "Right, now listen, this is what you have to do!" We had to carry the stone to a safe place where it could resonate or transmit the information out across the land.

At the same site, Joan had to convert some energy coming into the earth from above, into a frequency the earth could absorb. Her body's own energy pattern is designed to act as a filter for very powerful energies, and this is why she is on such a special frequency herself. She manipulates the energy with a series of movements, words and sounds which lower the frequency to the earth vibration and direct it to where it must go, usually to the earth-spirit at the core. On this occasion there were some beings from other planets in the area, working on the earth's etheric body, and to do that they needed the energy that Joan was filtering. We couldn't see the extra-terrestrials, because they were operating on a non-physical plane.

The second location, a potato field, involved something similar, though the energy here was even more powerful. Joan and John could actually see the energy coming down in flashes and spirals. We found the third spot among some large rocks near the summit of another hill. We stopped to have lunch. If they had a competition for the restaurant view of the world, this would come close! Our chairs were the rocks and our cuisine cheese sandwiches, but who cares among those hills and valleys! When we had finished, Joan said our bodies had been used in some way while we were eating and chatting. As we walked back down the hill, an arrow-shaped stone caught my attention, and whenever that happens I check with the pendulum. Yes, it said, I should take it. That was the fourth I had collected in a few days. I had been led to three others from the Burton Dassett Hills in Warwickshire.

A few miles down the road, as we were passing a small wood John asked me to stop the car quickly. We had been saying how beautiful it was, and our appreciation of the countryside had tuned John into the *Deva* frequency. The Devas are another form of evolution and the name comes from a Sanskrit word meaning 'Shining one'. They start their evolution by looking after individual plants and flowers and go on to guide groups of plants, a copse, a wood, an area of the countryside, a region, country, planet and so on. They are called *nature spirits* during their early stages and progress to become the archangels of the Bible stories.

Another aspect of the Deva evolution are the *elementals*, who work with the elements. Devas are spirit energy just as we are, but they might manifest themselves in a way humans expect or understand, and this is how the legends originate about fairies, gnomes, the little people, and angels with wings.

The Deva communicating with John said the wood might be beautiful, but it was tough trying to keep it like that, especially with the changes they were about to go through. We were asked to attract some energy to the wood from the earth-spirit, and we did this by visualisation. If you imagine something is happening, the thought-field thus created goes to work to achieve what you are visualising. Anyway, it worked and we left one happy Deva.

We thought the work was completed for the day, but on the way home John was keen to visit an ancient hill-fort in the area. Alongside it we found a BBC transmitter tower, and as we walked up the path we felt we were being pushed. In the end I was running. This was an important power centre and the transmitter was playing havoc with it. Human communications systems are doing tremendous harm to the energy grid. Some automatic writing said they were also making it more difficult to make contact across the dimensions. The human communications networks had:

> ...caused great problems for us as they have interfered with our communications channels, and we cannot allow this to continue. Consequently you will find that there will be severe disturbances with your communications systems, as we must clear channels to communicate with those who do our work. Your satellites are very basic and are not tuned to the correct frequencies for the work they do.

There was no doubt about the problems this transmitter was causing. You could almost feel the disharmony at the site. I had to walk around the outer circle of the fort in a clockwise direction while Joan and John cleared an energy-line going into the fort from the distant mountains. John was sure we had to go into the centre of the circle, which was not easy because it was covered by a wood. We ducked and weaved our way through to find a small mound. John was contacted by another Deva, the one with overall responsibility for the power centre. The transmitter had knocked the energy flow off-centre, and the Deva asked us to re-balance it. I walked around the outside of the mound while Joan and John went through their movements and sounds. Harmony was restored. "You are thrice blessed", said the Deva through John, "We now have the strength to face the transition".

On the way out I saw another stone, a lovely piece of slate, and again the pendulum said I should keep it. I was later told by a communication through John what I had to do with the stones I had collected. The ones I picked up in the Warwickshire hills were for Linda, Gareth and myself, and the arrow-shaped one was for Kerry. We would have to hold the stones assigned to us and they would give us information. We would have to do this three times before we assimilated all the knowledge, and I would know when to hand them out.

I have been led to many other stones. Some are for protection from the dark forces which seek to stop our evolution to a higher spiritual consciousness, others have helped me link up with spirit guidance, and others I have to take to different parts of the world to help to balance and harmonise vibrations between certain key energy-sites. I had to make one special trip to Scotland to find five stones on the shore of the River Tay. Three of these have to be taken across the world and two are to help me with my own development. I hope you can appreciate that stones are not just dead matter. Joan has some amazing crystals that do everything but talk to you, and our relationship with the mineral kingdom will be very different in the next century and beyond.

My journeys took me the length of England. I had to visit four of the seven English chakras on a main energy line across the country. The line runs from the south coast up through the Midlands to the northeast coast and off around the planet to complete the circle. The seven chakras on the English section of this ley-line or meridian are at the Needles Rocks off the Isle of Wight; the Iron Age fort at Uffington in Oxfordshire; Brailes Hill in Warwickshire; the site of Kenilworth Abbey; the ruins of Jervaulx Abbey in the Yorkshire Dales; the site of Durham Cathedral, and Staple Island, one of the Farne Islands. I had to visit the Needles, Uffington, Jervaulx and the Farne Islands.

I was due to pass near Uffington soon after I was given the messages, and so I went there first. It was a bright, sunny day, but as I neared the fort the sky began to cloud over. For the last few miles the sun was ahead of me, and rays of sunshine cascaded down spotlighting the landscape as if it were some giant stage. It was a rare sight. The Uffington Fort and the 'white horse' carved in the chalk on the hillside are tourist attractions, overlooking as they do the beautiful Vale of the White Horse. The 'fort' is a big circle with no stones, surrounded by a bank of earth with a path along the top.

I had been told I would know what to do, and I felt I should walk the circular path in a clockwise direction. The path is walked regularly by the visitors, but a number of people around the world, including myself, it would seem, have an energy pattern within our bodies which charges up the energies and the power-points in a certain way. When I had completed the circuit, I felt there was something more I had to do, and the pendulum supported that view. I remembered my visit to the stone circle in the Midlands, when I had to spiral across from one side to the other to re-charge my own energies. The pendulum agreed this was to be repeated here. As I moved across the centre in a turning motion, people were still walking around the perimeter path. They were thrown into sharp silhouette against the bright horizon just below the clouds. You would have thought this man spiralling across the circle would have attracted at least some interest, but no one took any notice.

The next day I was going to the Needles. I intended to go in the early evening because I was due to be at a local country show with the Green Party that day. But the rain poured all night and into the morning, an unusual event in a long, dry summer, and we decided not to attend. I was free to go to the Needles earlier. This was important because I realised when I arrived that the spot I needed to visit would have been locked up if I had gone when originally planned. I went up on to the headland leading down to the rocks. It is always a magnificent walk. The rain had stopped by now, there was little wind, and the views down to the famous coloured cliffs of Alum Bay and out across to the mainland were superb.

All was well until I'd got about half way, when the wind suddenly picked up dramatically, without warning. With that the rain was back, fierce and torrential, and I was drenched and dripping when I arrived at the Needles Battery, an old military base, now a museum. It is the nearest you can get to the rocks themselves, and I went to the fence at the far end and found myself looking out over the sea and down to the rocks and the red and white lighthouse. The Needles are three large rocks, on one of which the lighthouse stands. The second is close by, and, after a gap, the third stands, near to the headland. We had established that this third rock was the base chakra of the line as it passed across England. Again I had been given no instructions, only that I would know what to do. Well, walking around it was out for a start! The only words that came into my head were "Let there be light". I repeated the words many times, adding "Let the darkness be banished from this place".

After a few minutes, the pendulum confirmed the work was completed, and I went to the museum shop to buy a little guidebook. The Needles Battery was built as a defence against French invasion and had seen action during the last war. Many ships had also been wrecked in the bay. The pendulum spun a 'yes' when I asked if these events had created the negative energy I had been sent to clear. I cannot stress enough how important it is to know the consequences of dark thoughts. In the old days when there were guardians of the power-points, they would disperse such dark energy immediately it happened, but we have forgotten or ridiculed the old wisdoms, and so the energy has built up over many centuries.

I headed to Northumberland in the far northeast of England for my next stop on the energy-line, the chakra at Staple Island in the Farnes. These islands have a long spiritual tradition. Lindisfarne, or Holy Island, was an early centre of Christianity. St Aidan and St Cuthbert also had close associations with the Farnes in the Celtic period. The Farnes are named after a Celtic word meaning 'land'. I did not have to go to Staple Island: I could do what was necessary from the mainland shore. I walked down through the dunes to the expanse of sand between Seahouses and Bamburgh, looking out to some of the islands and the legendary Longstones Lighthouse. The pendulum led me to a spot near the water and I went through the same procedure that I did at the Needles. This time I also began to chant the ancient word I had been given in Kenilworth. Soon the pendulum was telling me the energy blockage was dispersed and I could go.

I completed my work on the line at Jervaulx Abbey in the Yorkshire Dales. I walked through a field of sheep to find the ruins of the Cistercian Abbey, which dates back to 1156. I dowsed a plan of the building in the guidebook to locate the chakra. It was an area of grass with two trees in the middle. There were several people around when I arrived, but a rain shower came at the right time and I was left alone to walk a circle around the trees. Confirmation was to come that evening that the work at the chakras had had the desired effect.

I went on from Jervaulx to meet the two psychics, John and Ian, who had also visited the Kenilworth source after her first communication. Ian's girlfriend June, another psychic, was there, too, along with the source and her husband. After a while the room became charged with energy, and as John closed his eyes a voice began to speak through him. The voice said we had been brought together that night because they knew we had many questions and they would try to answer them. The voice said there was "much shifting of gear and vibration". It said we must understand water with a wider perspective, and appreciate the energy carried in the water. The energies were to be changed. The three was to be replaced by the four. The three points of the triangle would become the four points of the diamond. Another kind of energy was being added which would transform life on earth. "There will be so many shifts, I find it difficult to explain them all to you".

The voice said the line through England had been cleared. "It is impossible for you to know how urgent this work has been – beyond your comprehension". The more we understood about the laws of the universe and the nature of life on earth, the less physical catastrophe had to occur, said the voice (that is, good thoughts can disperse bad ones and reduce the damage). This was why we, as humans, had a unique gift to decide our own futures. "If you understand this, you will truly become the gods that you ape on this planet".

The voice revealed that the line we had been clearing through England continued south from the Needles, through the Atlantic to South Africa, where there were many blockages. This was no surprise when you think of the dark thought-forms produced in that country for so long. "There is time", said the voice, "But the time is short". We were asked if we would "act as crystals for centres outside your solar system to clear this line". This involved all of us holding hands in a ring, and the energy being passed through us and into the line in South Africa. Each of us in the ring took on the energy for a few minutes as we made word-pictures for the rest of the group to focus on.

I remember June asked us to imagine the energy flowing through the sea and hitting a wall. We then imagined the wall being dismantled and the energy flowing through. I said we should picture the whole of South Africa as a brilliant light with all its people, black and white, throwing down their weapons and running to hug each other. At the end of each visualisation we would lift our hands and pass on the energy to the next person until the circle was complete. We were doing three things: dispersing dark thought-forms in South Africa which were affecting the line, acting as a filter to reduce the frequency of the energy to a form suitable for the earth to absorb, and projecting that energy by thought-fields to where it was needed. We must realise the power we all have in our possession to create and change through positive thought. The voice ended the communication by announcing that our efforts had succeeded.

There were encouraging signs in the various messages coming in, that The Plan was working well enough to ensure that the earth would survive the changeover, if the repairs to the energy grid continued apace throughout the world. And every improvement to the grid is reducing the physical consequences for humanity.

6

Lord of the Age

The symbolism of Judy Hall's spider in the web was beginning to make sense. I was in the privileged position of having information coming to me from many sources, and both the volume and the sources were about to expand substantially as the Plan revealed its global perspective. Some of the communications came from the consciousness which has the awesome responsibility of easing in and guiding the new age of Aquarius. This is Rakorczy, (pronounced Rakors-ski), known by many as the Lord of Civilisation and Lord of the Seventh Ray, one of the energies we will soon be receiving at a much increased power.

The universe is governed and guided by a massive hierarchy, and the personnel or consciousnesses are selected purely by a soul's stage of evolution. There are beings who guide the cosmic, galactic, solar and planetary systems, planets, countries, and regions. Each of these systems is broken down into further levels of organisation. At the head of our solar system is the Solar Logos, working with the Lords of the Rays who control the energies that affect the consciousness and spiritual development of life-forms. These have become known as *ascended masters*, and they are supported by other ascended masters, behind the scenes, as it were. It is not a case of the higher ordering the lower like some spiritual sergeant-major. Everyone has free will to agree or disagree.

Each ascended master like Rakorczy (some spell it Rakoczy) has what is called an ashram, a large group of souls on the physical and non-physical planes who work to a common purpose. A strategy is agreed before those assigned to work on earth incarnate for that life and, when the time is right, they are contacted. Gradually, the purpose of their incarnation seeps through to the brain as the knowledge is eased from their soul by experiences arranged for them by their colleagues on the spirit planes.

The Lords of the Rays are also known as The Great White Brotherhood, white being a reference to the forces of Light as opposed to darkness. They have enormous power and wisdom, and this is highlighted by the people they have been in their earth lives. It is claimed by some people that the Rakorczy consciousness has had incarnations as a ruler in the then–fertile Sahara 50,000 years ago, a high priest in Atlantis, Joseph (the father of Jesus), the prophet Samuel, Saint Alban, Merlin (King Arthur's 'magician'), the monk scientist Roger Bacon, the Count Saint-Germain of France, and... Francis Bacon.

Bacon was the son of Queen Elizabeth I and Robert Dudley, Lord Leicester, and was born four months after a secret wedding. He should have been king, but Elizabeth was determined to protect her status as the 'virgin queen' and to stop Dudley getting access to her wealth and power. She threatened her son with death if he revealed his true identity. Instead he was brought up by Sir Nicholas and Lady Anne Bacon – my soul's parents at the time – and became one of the greatest minds the Western world has produced. It was he, not Shakespeare, who wrote the famous plays. An aspect of this soul later returned as Count Saint-Germain, the man dubbed the 'Wonderman of Europe', in an unsuccessful attempt to bring democracy peacefully to France and Europe.

Rakorczy communicated with me at this stage through Joan in Wales. They had been working together for many years. On the first occasion I was there, Rakorczy told me something about my soul's history. I came to earth at the start of the Atlantis civilisation and I was there much later when it was destroyed by earthquakes, volcanoes and tidal waves. I went to the planet Mercury to begin my preparations for the task I have today. Each of my incarnations since then has been designed to prepare me for this time, and it is the same for everyone else who has a part to play in this transformation of consciousness and understanding.

An aspect of my soul had been a Welsh Celt, and this had been an important life because, said Rakorczy, "He sang like a bird to our will". No wonder I was so moved by those Welsh hills and valleys when I was out with Joan and John. "His soul revels in the ecstasy of its memories", as the ascended master put it.

Rakorczy had many other messages for me to ponder on that night, some personal, and others that would only become clear later:

> The diamonds can be found even in the mud – the waters wash them clean. Nuggets of gold (philosophy) are not for you. Seek diamonds, sparkling truth, the clarity, perfection of the Word. The whirlpools of life carry you to where the diamonds are. Resonate to the perfection of the crystals. Arduous seeking is not necessary. The path is already mapped out. You have only to follow the clues.

> The race against time is of some importance, but the standard of the work is of greater importance. If any urgency arises, you will be told. Do not worry. Learn to relax – there is always tomorrow. Every physical life needs pleasure and enjoyment. Don't ever forget humour. We are guiding you along a set path. You are learning according to our teaching of you. It was all organised before you incarnated.

I had been concerned about my family during the upheavals because I knew we would be apart for long periods, but Rakorczy eased my mind:

> No need to worry about your wife. She has a job to do. Leave her free to do it without any worries, any strings, any attachments, so, like a bird she can fly off whenever she will and

back to you whenever she's able, and you to her.

Your son is his own self and must go his own way. He has his path and it is no concern of yours. You are merely his custodians while he is young. One day your daughter will see her star and go for it.

None of you realise how much the love for the Godhead enfolds you. It cares and guides. Not one single being is left alone, uncared for. All is gathered in at the end of the day, and not one sheep will be left in the field.

True love does not always give the receiver what it would like to receive, but it will always give that which is best for it. So welcome everything you receive whether you like it or not. Ponder on anything you do not like and see if you can see why it was necessary. Acceptance will then be very much easier.

I can report the words, yes, but the love and warmth that came over was indescribable. We may have a lot of challenges to face, but there are some wonderful beings on our side doing all they can to help.

One of Rakorczy's team was communicating through automatic writing to a sensitive in Northamptonshire. I became aware of her when she was asked by her communicator to pass on some messages to the Kenilworth source. I arranged to see her, and she was taking automatic writing almost to the moment I knocked at her door. Only a minute or two earlier the messages had ended with the words "I will stop now as your visitor is close!"

Her communicator was 'Attarro, Avatar of the Alchemians'. An avatar is a much evolved being, and alchemy is the transformation of the spirit to a higher understanding. Attarro, along with a host of beings from other stars and planets, has come to the earth in, for the moment, a non-physical form. One message explained their role:

We have been waiting to reach your planet for a long time. I come to you as a friend and wish to give you the truths. I have come to understand much from my planetary existence and I am here to protect Mother Earth. She speaks to me in language that earthlings are too deaf to hear. I come in peace. My work must not be misinterpreted, as I am here to link the puzzle pieces during the next decade to the year 2000.

Attarro confirmed the problems facing the earth as the change-over approaches, when one type of energy would be replaced by another, more powerful energy of a higher frequency and quicker vibration. There surround many cosmoses, each reaching out indefinitely, but linking together to form a mass which is interlinked like a vortex of many lines. These lines are linked to the earth, and the ley-lines are like the veins of the universe, pumping blood to the planet. We should imagine a grid system, not only transversing the earth, but also interlacing all our planets and suns as one great electrical system. Ley-lines, as they are being destroyed, are imbalancing the cosmos, and the earth is in danger of being cut off from her heavenly brothers and sisters. The avatars had been sent to help before the links are cut off completely and Mother Earth is lost. The Earth is a pulse point of great energy within God's Light and world, and God had no wish to lose this child of light and love. If the earth were lost, so a cosmos would fold with her, and this could not be allowed to happen.

A Black Sabbath was about to arrive out of the heavens and make colossal changes. Only by people learning to sing in harmony could they relieve the apparent dismal events. Disease and disharmony would stifle the earth over the next decade, leaving space only for the spiritually strong and influential, and more so the pure in heart, who would win through triumphantly. When I read this I thought of that Biblical prediction 'The meek shall inherit the earth'. The Avatar said the keys to the universe were being dangled in front of the humans' third eye, which we had to open to enter the next stage, the new realisations, all the things that were due to come.

Much will be learned, blood will be shed, through Man's own fault, and the next few years will see such changes.

Mother Earth is choking, and as she coughs and wheezes, the earth will open up through land shifts. As she cries so the land will be flooded. Volcanoes will erupt, all to cleanse our Mother. Many new scars have appeared on our earth. Energy lines are being broken through new roads which interfere with sacred ground, which was dwelt upon by our animals who love, nurture, and trust nature, and who live totally within their natural cycle and habitat, able to understand nature's simple messages.

The time has arrived when many people would begin to feel a change in their hearts. This is because the new vibration is beginning to take effect. This would force human consciousness up to the next rung. There were many tribespeople who read nature well. They had told, and would tell again, of the imminent changes. The skies would appear darker and the equinoxes appear different to that of the star scholar. What we know as a comet would be seen in the night sky.

Attarro said the Earth had great love and devotion for the human form, but she could not survive the pressures being imposed upon her. The Earth was trying to communicate her knowledge to us, and this explained the mystery of the crop circles, the strange shapes that have appeared in corn fields all over the world. They began as a series of perfect circles, but during 1990, as this story started to unfold, in parts of England they became very detailed, with amazing shapes and patterns. Scientific attempts to explain this phenomenon from within the sphere of current knowledge convinced few, including, I suspect, many of the scientists. Attarro named the being responsible – the Earth herself. The shapes were formed by energy from below.

These rings are of great importance... the energy is transmuting, and the symbols rise from the voice of the Earth. Just by taking shape they reach our inner eyes and memories, and for those who glance or are aware, they reach deeply to send the quiet messages of Mother Earth. The vibrance of these areas can be measured. Crystals laid on these areas will absorb a subtle energy and help to transmute and communicate messages which are hidden from our memories.

The symbols and the duality of nature are reaching to the heavens to transmit their energies out to skies which are desperately breaking down their chemical composition, due to pollution. Rings will spring up in many unexpected places. They may appear through rock formations and even in water through the synergy of currents. The circles are to amend the lost power and unblock ley-lines which are in trouble. The lines and the format surrounding them are like an echo-system to extend the transmission and power.

We should notice, said Attarro, the vortices and angles in the crop patterns. Many of the shapes, if fitted together, would give a deeper meaning. From a great height Creation would perceive these as a mass pattern, not individual crop shapes. The whole area should be likened to a giant canvas which is being etched to draw planetary influences and healing to Mother Earth, who is struggling to keep her natural balance. The Earth is a sublime creature herself, with a consciousness that does not forget any detail, but absorbs each and every event, pain, joy and destruction of any of her creatures.

She tries to reach us in many ways, but now is the time to communicate her deeper level of consciousness. Her messages are simple, her language complete. It just needs decoding. Through the absorption of her symbols, so the message, like beautiful music, plays deeply within our souls.

These symbols, said Attarro, had been etched many times on stone walls throughout civilisation, and it is not the first time they had appeared on nature's canvas. It is necessary to rock human awareness, as it became self-absorbed and not part of the divine family. So there you have the many reasons for crop circles: to send out energy to help the polluted skies and ozone layer, to draw in other healing energy for the Earth, to boost flagging ley-lines, and to use symbols to awaken the memory of the soul. Symbols can be very powerful. Some symbols given to the source of this communication came with a warning only to show them to the spiritually aware, because they could be dangerous for others. It is also interesting to note that language experts approached for the view on the crop shapes said they looked like the symbols of the ancient Sumerians, which supports what Attarro said.

The poor condition of the energy-system was revealed when the Avatar talked about Avebury, the stone circles in Wiltshire, England. I was guided there to walk the circles, and I was astonished to see a village had been built on the site, with a road going through the middle of the circles. No wonder it is in a mess. Avebury is one of the earth's major chakras, but the Avatar said it is open and bleeding, and a 'whirlpool of festering pus'. Many people would need to chant to heal the damage. New stones should be laid to replace those that had been lost, and existing stones had to be healed by seven healers harmonising together. There had been much folly at this site, especially in the last 50 years, and many sexual rites had been held in this area, which 'feed the pool with deeper pus'. The damage at Avebury was mirrored throughout the world as many sacred lands were desecrated:

> Areas with sacrificial negativity are once again upon us with fighting and hatred. Consecrated ground is being built on, not for temples, but for pointless meanderings which will cascade down in a few short years. My friends, find the consecrated ground around you, make it clean again with your efforts. Expose the charlatans and the money-mongers and keep the grounds and the rocks pure.

Attarro said the greatest enemy of the planet was that of our thoughts and deeds. It was the dark energy we were producing in this way that was the weapon for the Earth's destruction. That was not to say chemical disorder is not a major problem – it is. But much work is needed on our emotional and mental state.

> Now is the time of dramatic change, a time to unclutter our lives of materialism, to give us the space we need to breath, to cleanse our thoughts and our actions...

> Keep your hearts pure. Joy can be as catching as anything. Go

about your work with a joyous heart, exude love and wisdom and principle. Speak the truth to those you can listen, and even to those who do not wish to listen. The seeds of truth will bury and in time will grow.

Healing was frequently the subject of the Avatar's letters, especially healing through colour, and many times the lost civilisation of Atlantis was mentioned. There would be many breakthroughs when the healing knowledge of Atlantis returned after the transformation into the next age. Surgery with a knife would be outmoded. Only the use of hands, colour, crystals, and waters would be necessary. A new pioneer would vocalise wondrous findings which were just the innate memories of his ancestors. Unfortunately, he may be laughed at, and it could be another 50 years before the ideas began to be used. The use of colour for healing is already emerging. Each colour is a frequency of the energy, and if you get the right colour and frequency for the right complaint, you can restore harmony to the body and emotions.

We look upon modern medical science with understandable wonder, from the limitations of our current knowledge and awareness. But in fact cutting bits out of people, organtransplantation, toxic drug therapy and so on, is the medical dark ages. The future lies in prevention and cure through the energy-fields. This is beginning very slowly to emerge under the heading of 'Vibrational Medicine'[1]. Although some practitioners do not realise it, we already have vibrational medicine at work in what is known as homoeopathy. Few people can understand why diluting a plant extract again and again can possibly have any power over disease, but in fact the vibration of the plant is still present in the water and it is the vibration, not the substance, of the homoeopathic preparation that has the effect on illness.

There were many warnings from the Avatar about nuclear technology, and medicine and science: "I try hard not to feel angry at the nonsense man has made. All is simple magic before your eyes. Don't mess with genetics, just blend the substances given to you on Earth". Chemistry was simple, as all laws were. We should work *with* them, not against them. We should work with the flow of the planet, encourage and enjoy the elements and encourage and learn from the seasons. "Look for the simplicity and synchronicity around you. For everything there is a duality, and somewhere within it the answer lies. All is equal. When one (polarity) tries to rule the other only war and pain and ills proceed. When each lives in harmony, all strife will cease, and the planet and the cosmos will unite. The choice is yours".

Attarro often talked about the Bible. Even though it had been changed and misinterpreted, it still held many answers, and many secrets were revealed. The Bible had been written by alchemists, magicians, seers, healers and doctors, who themselves had written of things they did not understand. They had left them for their children to follow. We should let the Bible fall open, using the old text and not the revised versions, as many secrets have been lost. The tombs of time were opening, the cobwebs clearing and the sun arising. We should also hold our religious ceremonies outside in the elements, preferably within the gentle magnetism of the stones. Worshipping indoors under a roof was too restricting and diminished the effect.

The knowledge, wisdom and advice of the Avatar covered many varied subjects as the sensitive's pen flowed to the rhythm of the thought-forms. This is a summary of some of it:

Only plants, shrubs and vegetation which have been grown in the soil of a country for 50 years are suitable for the inhabitants of that country. The planet's balance is for the gentle use of humans, and too much importation of goods, natural and manufactured, disrupts the natural balance of each continent's vibrations. We should use where found or made as much as possible. Waters and rivers preserve the natural energies of the universe. Rock crystals and quartz are part of the chemistry to keep the unison flowing. Coal and charcoal should be left in the earth where they filter the waters down into the core, keeping the earth moist and cool and at the correct temperature for humans to live on. Colour and mystical music cure many ills, including heart disease and cancer, which are caused by stress and are bio-chemically related. The techniques would also transform childbirth and give the child a more serene beginning. The moment of birth, as Atlantis had taught, should be a delight for mother and child, not full of fear, trepidation and trauma. The use of lights, water and serene music has been lost in the tidal wave of humanity's greed and materialism.

I learned much from these messages, and many blurred areas were brought into focus. I learned more about myself, too, in a message sent by Attarro, the day I went to see the Northamptonshire sensitive for the first time. It said I always had three spirit beings around me to guide and protect me, and only good could come from my work. (I was told later that my three guides are from the planet Uranus.) I was also told that I might become involved in literature about the Incas of Peru, and that I should let my vibration flow in that direction. I would be drinking of holy water soon and meeting with people of great importance through my work. Many mystics would gather and a new group would be born.

Attarro said the sensitive would know me by my eyes, my voice, and the shape of my fingers (swollen through arthritis), and that she may see other things around me and be aware of my unusual energy-patterns. "He is a solidifier of thought and helps the Word to surface with those he meets". She should tell me to go east and put my mind and thoughts in that direction. I should "meet with the dragon soon" (subsequently confirmed as Japan). I would have to write several difficult letters (I already knew what some of these would be), but my hand would flow when the time was ripe.

The channel was widening, said Attarro, and the information was ready to pour. My work-place might change shape or position unexpectedly and then much truth would be found. As she took this part of the message, the sensitive had the vision of a ginger cat. I was about to leave for Canada and I was told my timetable there might be slightly disrupted. I was warned to take care of my own health and that of Linda. "She is rather over-tired of late, and a little swallowed by the change of events. We send our love and blessings to her also, as she is the bowl and you are the roses". There might be a time when I was "led on". I should watch for the time, it would be around the daffodils. "Watch your signature on the paper – and know the dealer and the dealings".

Later that afternoon the sensitive gave me a reading with Tarot cards. I had to select a pile of cards from the pack at random, and she was given psychic messages based upon the symbols of the cards I had chosen. She said I would meet some sort of doctor. This would happen when I was not expecting to meet anyone. There would be a lot of information coming through this person, or he or she would lead me to people with information. She asked me if I had been working on the story of the Holy Grail, the famous legend about King Arthur's, Merlin's and the Knights of the Round Table's search for this object. I had. I already knew from other communications that the story was true and the characters had existed, and I knew that an aspect of Rakorczy had been Merlin. There have been many theories about what the Grail actually is. Some say a chalice cup made from the cross on which Christ was crucified, and others say it was a stone. The sensitive said the truth of the legend would be made known to me soon.

She went on to say that the next six months would show incredible changes in me; I would have a different energy-flow and my feminine vibration, the one that governed intuition and psychic abilities, would be tuned up. I would be given a talisman in the next two months which would be a good vibration for me to hold or to wear. There would be travel to all ends of the earth, much of which would be on water. I would spend several months in different places, and she said there was a strong Australian feel. (A trip to Australia has since been confirmed by another psychic.)

All the expanding sources of information were confirming and cross-checking each other on the basic story of reincarnation, karma, the energy-system, the great changes for people and the earth, and the job I am here to do. All were telling the same tale, and it would not be long before many of the predictions by Rakorczy, the Avatar and the sensitive were all to be proved right by events.

7

Diamonds in the Mud

Deborah Shaw had returned to Canada, and a connection with the North American Indians was emerging strongly. They, too, carried the knowledge of the energy-system through the generations, but much of it has been lost as their culture has become Westernised.

In the days before she left Kenilworth to return to Alberta, Deborah was getting psychic messages and visions about a past life as a member of the Blackfoot Tribe, which is still based a short drive from her home in Calgary. Every time she closed her eyes on her return flight she saw Indians standing, walking or dancing. She was told that her Indian life ended in the last century at the age of 98. The Indians revered their elders and her age alone made her special to them with all the knowledge she had of the old ways. Apparently, she had natural healing powers in that lifetime, but they were suppressed by some emotional blockage.

Two days after this information came through to her, she was busy on the phone as one call followed another. But then she felt an enormous push and she was left in no doubt that she should leave the phone, sit down, and clear her mind for a message. It said that I had to go to Alberta and an area south of

Calgary near the site of the Old Man River Dam – a dam which the Indians had unsuccessfully opposed, because it meant flooding part of their sacred burial grounds. Deborah said the clarity of the message was the most powerful she had yet received.

She wrote to me with the details of the communication, and within a week another letter had arrived. She had been given a further message. She had seen a vision of an Indian who was in a boat with the body of a woman. He shot an arrow into the air and it was guided by the Great Spirit and landed in a special place. It was here that the woman was laid to rest. She was very special and so was he. Both Deborah and myself were in the vision also. The Indians in the scene were obviously from another age, but the surroundings were modern, how they would look today.

I had no doubt that I should go. I was speaking at an Animal Rights Conference in the United States a month later, and I arranged to spend the previous week in Calgary. When I met Deborah at the airport neither of us knew what was going to happen or where we were to go, although her rapidly developing psychic abilities provided a good link with the spirit guides and I was sure all would be well.

Deborah grew up in the English Midlands in the Kenilworth/Leamington area. Both her parents died when she was young. One day when she was in her teens the soul of her mother contacted her. She thought she was losing her mind, and it took many years and a visit to a medium for her to accept that she was psychic and that what she was seeing was real. By the time we met at Calgary Airport, the communication channel was so open she was constantly seeing spirit-forms.

She took me to the Glenbow Museum in Calgary, where one floor is devoted to Indian history. There were many mentions of shamans and medicine men, who were keepers of the knowledge in each tribe, passing this knowledge on only to those who were trusted. Even then they had to go through a long apprenticeship. We found a picture at the exhibition of an un-named Indian chief holding copies of treaties signed with the white settlers in the last century. We both dowsed that my soul had been that chief.

We were also led to many books. At the museum shop we

bought one about Indian history, and I was particularly struck by a picture of a medicine wheel. This was the Indian version of a stone circle, an energy-power point. The Indians would dance around them to charge up the energy, and the sounds they made would do the same. At another shop in the city we were led to other books, including one called *Star People* about people alive on Earth today who came from other planets, and another called... *Medicine Wheels*. These were obviously going to play a major part in this visit to Canada.

The next stop on this spiritually-guided tour was the junction of two rivers in Calgary, the Bow and the Elbow. This is close to the Calgary Fort Historic Park, where the white settlers first made their home in what was to become the present-day city. It was hard to believe, looking across at the skyscrapers of downtown Calgary, that this settlement was established in the lands of the Indians little more than 100 years ago. It has been said several times in communications that rivers are vitally important to the energy-system and the life of the earth, and the points where rivers meet are especially powerful. This power had been diminished at the junction of the Bow and Elbow by the anger and resentment of the Indians at seeing their way of life destroyed. This had produced much dark energy, as had the settlers with their treatment of the Indians.

We had to sprinkle water symbolically from the rivers on to the land and say whatever came into our minds or, rather, what was put into them. Deborah said: "Forgive them everything", and I said once again: "Let there be light". This spot is symbolic in itself of what we have done to the world in such a tiny speck of time. We looked in one direction and saw the beauty of the Bow as it hurried out of the city. We looked the other way and there was modern Calgary, with its pillars of glass standing in worship and homage to the god they call oil.

We were led by the pendulum to the top of the mound that once was Fort Calgary. I thought this might be an energy-centre which we were meant to clear. Instead, there was a ceremony to perform to remove one of my own karmic blocks. Deborah was given the words I had to say: "I forgive myself for all the wrongs I have done in all my past lives. I forgive all those who have hurt me or will try to hurt me in the future. To err is human, to forgive divine".

It was becoming obvious that I had some kind of link with the Indians in this area of Canada, and this was confirmed the following day when we went to Nose Hill high above Calgary. The views are spectacular, but it has become a bit of a dumping ground for debris and earth from building sites. We climbed one of these mounds of earth, which had grassed over, and the message came that we should face the sun and chant the ancient words we had each been given. We then had to give thanks for the privilege of being in such a sacred place, and ask for courage and strength for what we had to do in the future. Deborah said we were surrounded by the spirit-forms of Indians. They said if we spoke to them they would hear and respond. I said how much I respected their wisdom and knowledge and how determined I was to see the truth win through. They said we were "a true brother and sister of the family".

They told us that another mound nearby covered the site of a medicine wheel, a very powerful energy-site, and we had to walk a circle seven times to charge it up as best we could. The communications were coming mainly from an Indian spirit who took the form of an elder, and he had, Deborah said, "a twinkle in his eye". He described the wonderful life they had before the land was taken away. They were sad, but not bitter at how they and the land had been treated. But, he told us, the great wind would blow away the mounds of earth and all would be restored. "The winds will move boulders as if they are pebbles", he said.

The next afternoon, we travelled some distance from Calgary near to another point where two rivers meet. We had to walk quite a way along the side of a river and then climb on to a ridge looking out across the country. It was a place of indescribable beauty, known by the ancient Indians as Long Shadows. On the ridge, the pendulums were spinning very strongly in the negative direction, indicating a serious energy-imbalance. We didn't know quite what to do and Deborah asked for guidance. The message came immediately that we should go down on to a small plain below the ridge. As soon as we arrived I saw some bushes. I knew that was the spot, and Deborah felt the same.

It was the site of an old medicine wheel and Indian camp.

The wheels were made of small stones arranged like a wagon wheel, with lines of stones going from the circle to a central point. The stones were aligned to the earth's energies, astrological movements and principles. They go back thousands of years. Another host of Indian spirits appeared to Deborah to tell the story of this place. The settlement had been joyous and happy until the son of the chief had destroyed something sacred to them in a moment of defiance. They decided to kill him, and this had taken place on the ridge we had just left. After that the life-energy of the tribe had ebbed away and they broke up in pain, anger and bitterness. The time had come to remove the pain, re-unite the tribal family, and forgive the soul of the son which had been through much suffering. It was also time to restore the life-force to this area.

We walked the circle of the former medicine wheel seven times as instructed and went back to the ridge. There, under spiritual direction, we had to hold hands to form a circuit of energy and ask the Great Spirit to cleanse the site and offer forgiveness to the soul of the son. I said that the period of pain and suffering was over and the soul was welcomed back into the arms of the family. All was forgiven and we should look ahead with joy and hope to the new world that was soon to come. "Let the pain and suffering be gone and the light flow again", I said, and Deborah was given the words: "And the deer will drink the water, the children will laugh, and families will be re-united".

When it was over Deborah saw the spirit-form of an eagle with a red eye flying over us. He said we would always have his protection, always be under his wing. As we left, the spirits of the Indians said they were getting their head-dresses on and they were going to have a big celebration party. All these activities were happening on the astral plane, but the karmic consequences of their earth-lives had to be broken by a ceremony on the plane where the events took place, and the energy blockage had to be dispersed on this plane, also, which was why we had to be there.

As we made our way back, my attention was taken by a stone on the ground, and the pendulum said I should take it with me. It was, we subsequently discovered, one of the stones that once made up the medicine wheel. I have to take it to a major energy-site in Asia. On the outward journey we had to climb a fence, and we remembered it well because it was none too easy. When we returned there, however, there was a little black stone on the top of the fence, which had definitely not been there before. This was the talisman the sensitive had predicted, and I was told to keep it with me always. On the other side of the fence was a stone left for Deborah. Other predictions by the Avatar and the sensitive also came true: when I first arrived at Deborah's house, I met her cat. It was ginger. And my Canadian time-table was slightly disrupted – I had to stay on an extra day.

By now I knew more about my soul's past life as an Indian. I had been Setting on an Eagle Tail, the chief of the Peigan Indians (pronounced Paygan), who were linked together with some other tribes under the name Blackfoot. He was chief from 1875 until his death ten years later, and he signed the peace treaty with the settlers along with other chiefs. Linda, Kerry and Gareth were all with me in that life.

The name Blackfoot – which resulted from the colour of their moccasins – was given to one individual tribe as well as being an overall term for several. The next afternoon we were directed to the Blackfoot reservation and their burial grounds. Under a large cross we found the grave of Crowfoot, one of the most famous Canadian Chiefs, who also signed the peace treaties. There, Deborah picked up a piece of seemingly dead wood with a round hole in the centre, and the pendulum indicated that I should take it home.

Our other call at the reservation was at the college, where there is a small museum of original Blackfoot clothes and artifacts. It was late afternoon and we were told at the college that we were too late.

The museum was closed, they said, and locked up for the day. This was a blow, but we decided to see if the curator was still around. There was no reply when I knocked on his office door, and we were about to leave when I saw another door ajar. It was dark inside, but as I found the light we saw that we were standing in the museum. Someone had forgotten to lock up. We were drawn to the medicine bags used by the medicine men –

they were generating terrific power. Apparently, they were giving us a form of protection. For some reason I have yet to establish, I also had to write down Eagle Tail's Indian name, which was printed on a copy of the peace treaty in the museum. It was Zaotze Tapitapiw.

That evening we visited the home of a lovely Canadian lady who was going to introduce us to an Indian friend. But we soon realised that it was her, not the Indian friend, whom we were meant to see. She had many books on spiritual and mystical matters, and they, along with our conversation, gave us a number of clues. Deborah was looking at a book of mystical pictures called *Shaman, the Paintings of Susan Sedden-Boulet,* and in it she found a picture of Merlin holding a piece of wood exactly like the one we found at Crowfoot's grave. The words alongside the painting said:

I will not forget these stones that are set,
In a round on Salisbury Plain,
Tho' who brought 'em there, 'tis hard to declare,
The Romans, or Merlin, or Danes.

A few days after my return to England I had to take the piece of wood and bury it at a round on Salisbury Plain. It wasn't Stonehenge, but I won't say where it was because it is balancing the vibrations, I understand, between that site and the one in Canada, and must be left alone.

Later during that evening, the lady began to talk about obsidian, a volcanic rock. Even she didn't know why she suddenly brought this into the conversation, but it proved to be significant. She showed us a book which said obsidian was normally found in areas of present or past volcanic activity and was formed in the same way as is a diamond. It was a protection stone, and helped to safeguard the owner from being emotionally drained by others. It gave support for those stressed by outside pressures and protected the soft-hearted and gentle people of the world from being misused. Its very colour, black, acted as a screen to keep out the unwanted, said the book. The talisman I had been given is made from obsidian.

There were enough mentions of a certain crystal shop that

night to leave us in no doubt that we were to go there. At the shop we were led to a book about a stone called moldovite. We both had to buy a copy, and a piece of moldovite came free with each one. The exact origin of the stone isn't known except that it came down to earth from somewhere else in the universe and landed in what is now Slovakia about 14.8 million years ago. It is thought to help to accelerate spiritual awakening, and has been linked with the legend of the Holy Grail. We talked with the shop owner as we bought the books, and in the course of that conversation he mentioned various places in Alberta, including Vulcan. The moment he said the name it struck a strong and immediate chord with both of us. We knew there was something to be done in that area, and away we went to start what was to be the longest day of our lives.

Vulcan is only a small settlement, and by Canadian standards only a short drive from Calgary. As we got closer a cloud ahead of us became a spectacular tapestry of colour. All the other clouds in the sky were white, but this one was red, blue, green, gold, every colour you could think of. While this was happening our attention was caught by the sharp, black silhouette of a figure standing at the top of a large mound to our right. The pendulum was most emphatic that this was the place we should stop. When we pulled over, Deborah had a vision of purply-green rocks pulsating inside the mound. We walked to the top and there was no sign of anyone. The dark figure had been projected by the spirit-realms simply to point out the spot.

We were told that the bodies of many murdered Indians were buried in the mound and, as a result, it was beset with dark energy. We had to remove and keep two large stones buried in the summit, and perform a ceremony with water to allow the energy of Light to flow again and disperse the darkness. We had bought a bottle of water 20 minutes earlier with the intention of drinking it. We were led from here to the place where two rivers meet on the plains nearer to Calgary, or, more to the point, where two rivers appeared to meet when we looked at the map. Those rivers had now been sucked dry by the demands of the monoculture cornfields that have turned this once-beautiful area into a featureless, soulless monument to human misunderstanding.

We found our location in a large field alongside what was once a river. Again, it was beset with dark energy. A communication to Deborah told of the time when an Indian tribe lived here. Many of them had died of smallpox after being given blankets by white traders which had once covered smallpox victims. Sometimes this was done by accident, but it was also used as a way of wiping out tribes so their land and few possessions could be taken. The medicine man of that tribe had suffered great anguish when he could not cure his people. This was a white man's disease and he had no answer to it. The soul of the medicine man was still suffering, and there was another ceremony of forgiveness to perform to clear the energy blockages. Deborah had to sprinkle soil on to a stone.

A little further up the road, or track as it was, there was another site to clear, part of what had been the same Indian settlement. Deborah began to feel pains in her shoulders and left side. Here an elder of the tribe had put a curse on the land and we had to remove the curse for the sake of the land and the soul responsible. The elder had been racked with pain at the end of his earth-life, and this related to what Deborah was feeling. I had to put my hand on these areas of pain and ask the Great Spirit to free the soul and the land from the consequences of the curse. Immediately her pain disappeared. Deborah saw a vision of the elder riding off into the distance, free at last.

It was late afternoon and we had been out for six hours. We asked if we were finished for the day. No, came the reply. Finished? We had hardly begun. We were guided west and towards the foothills of the Rocky Mountains. Our first stop was a place called Magnetic Hill. From there you can see a massive area of land down across the plains and up over the foothills to the Rockies. We found a cattle trough carved out of a tree trunk, and this was where another Indian had laid a curse on all the land he could see in response to the activities of the settlers. Another ceremony of forgiveness and release was performed for the soul and the land.

As we travelled deeper and deeper into the hills and forests, Deborah was getting more information about these curses. Three brothers and two of their wives had decided to curse as much of the land the white man was taking as they possibly

could. One brother had been the elder on the horse at the
smallpox camp, another had been the Indian at the water trough
on Magnetic Hill, and one of the wives had been the soul of
Deborah. The other brother was the spirit she had said had a
twinkle in his eye at Nose Hill. That spirit had once been her
husband.

We travelled for many miles through the forests, much of it
on dirt roads, until we were told to stop. This was where
Deborah's soul and the other wife in the story had stood back-
to-back and cursed all the land they could see in both directions.
It was what the Indians called bad medicine. Deborah's mother
had been telling her for days to learn the words of the song 'I
Vow to Thee My Country', and now she knew why. She had to
sing it at this spot! She could just about remember the main
words between laughing. This was, of course, merely symbolic
of her soul saying sorry and asking forgiveness for what it had
done. With that, the bad medicine was lifted and a blockage was
removed which would allow her psychic powers to become
even stronger. It was this same blockage that suppressed her
natural healing powers during that Indian life. Her mother
confirmed that she would become even more psychic from now
on. "You will start to see things happen now", she said. Deborah's mother had other personal reasons to ensure that the
freeing of this land went well. She had been the other Indian
wife who had imposed the curse.

Night fell, and the moon appeared magnificently over the
trees. It was the night before full moon, and the landscape
glowed with its reflection. We were heading for another place,
for something I had to do. We had established that in the life
that I became Chief Eagle Tail, I had known the Indian woman
who was Deborah, and she had taken every opportunity to
encourage me to hate the white man. We were asked to stop the
car alongside a river which winds its way through the hills. I had
been gifted with so many memorable sights on my travels, but
this was the finest yet. The moon was reflecting its power on the
surface of the river and backlighting the hills. There was not a
sound, save the odd vehicle passing. We walked along the river
bank, stopping many times to admire the moon's perfect image
on the water.

Eventually we came to a place where the path went right to the water's edge and opened out to form a small ridge. The next stage of the story came through. I had signed the treaty with the settlers, but while we saw it as a peace treaty between nations, they saw it as a real estate contract. Once we were on the reservations we became little more than prisoners, and we had to battle to keep even the land the treaties had allocated to us. One night I had tricked the tribe medicine man into giving me the means to put bad medicine on this land, and I had come to this spot because this was where the soul of Deborah had met her husband, and she had told me about its beauty many times.

I had to ask the Great Spirit for forgiveness, to forgive myself, and to ask for the curse on the land to be lifted. I said I had learned that hatred and resentment were not the answers, whatever the provocation. Only forgiveness and unconditional love for all could solve the problems of the earth and its people. I walked away from that unforgettable place, my soul lightened by the burden of karma that I had now left behind.

We were several hours from home already, but there was still much more to do. We saw a sign to the construction site for the Old Man River Dam, and as this had been part of Deborah's first message for me, we turned off. We went across a bridge over the river and stopped at one of the entrances to the site. As we did so Deborah said: "This is it – this is the scene I saw in the vision".

The river was low, and we walked across the mud and thousands of large stones to the water-side. When we stopped I saw a stone shaped like a diamond; the pendulum said we should take it with us. Then I saw another diamond-shaped stone and another and another. We collected eleven, and the words of Rakorczy came back to me: "The diamonds can be found even in the mud – the waters wash them clean, the whirlpools of life (those Indian incarnations) will lead you to where the diamonds are".

Deborah was given the background to her vision of the Indians in the boat. It was something that had happened 1400 years ago. Her soul had been the woman in the boat – she was the medicine woman of the tribe. The man who fired the arrow had been the chief and her husband – he was the soul of the lady we had met the night before in Calgary. My soul had been their son. Where the arrow had landed in Deborah's vision was now the burial ground held sacred by the present-day Indians, who were campaigning against the building of the dam, which would flood the area. We had to perform another ceremony, again sprinkling the water on the land to remove symbolically the effects of past and present events.

We were told the diamond stones would be used to make a form of medicine wheel on Nose Hill the following night. As we drove towards Calgary we were being asked to stop at almost every by-road off the main highway to clear energy-blockages. Deborah would get pains in her back, leg, arm or wherever, and she would be told of incidents of horrific cruelty that happened at the various places. All the victims were Indians. They had been shot, beaten, raped, disabled – the stories were appalling. We lost count of the number of times we had to stop. At each place we had to ask the Great Spirit (a perfect description of the Godhead) to forgive the souls who did the deed, and the soul of the victim for the hatred and resentment that resulted from it. What a sad place this area must have been. Deborah had a message that Michael or Mikaal, the archangel responsible for the earth, was working with us that night. We were also told that the forces of darkness were trying to disrupt our work.

It was clear as we got nearer to Calgary that all these locations were on a ley-line going into Nose Hill which, our spirit-guides told us, is one of the seven major chakras on the earth's emotional body. It is the equivalent to the human body's forehead or third eye chakra, the one through which we develop spiritual awareness. Canada is an energy-centre of world importance, with chakras on all of the earth's bodies. England has two earth chakras, one at Glastonbury Tor in Somerset and another at Avebury in Wiltshire, and some of the world's most famous landmarks are also chakras or major energy sites, including Uluru or Ayers Rock in Australia.

It was nearly five o'clock in the morning when we reached Nose Hill and looked out over the blaze of neon that was Calgary. Here we had to ask the Great Spirit to forgive all the souls who had ever lived in this area for all the wrongs they had done to each other, and to disperse the shields of darkness with the power of Light. We both had to speak these words three times. When we arrived home, we had been out for 20 hours.

There was one other aspect to that night which gave us what seemed to be a glimpse of some of the star movements that will, we were told, soon take place. At several of our stops, Deborah was sent a vision relating to the future. She saw the earth as an egg-timer with the sand running out, and then came news of changes in the night sky:

> The star constellations appeared as their astrological symbols. Taurus the Bull changed its position in relation to Pegasus the Horse. They started out looking away from each other and turned to face one another. Three shields appeared carrying the symbols of the horse, lion and bear, representing the constellations of Pegasus, Leo and the Great Bear. The bear jumped over the top of the horse, indicating the constellations will change places accordingly.

> She saw the lady, which is the symbol of the constellation Cassiopeia, looking between the two lines of Gemini. The bear then moved through between the two lines.

> A few days later she saw the lion turn upside down and a beam of light coming to the earth from Regulus, a star in the Leo constellation.

With these visions came the message that the new energy-system cannot reach the earth with the stars in their present positions and these, therefore, would change. All would begin in 1992 with the process complete by 1998. It will be, she was told, the 31st or 32nd century before evidence of these changes can be seen from earth.

The energies are stepped down in frequency at the various levels so that no planet receives energy it cannot handle. If we, at our stage of evolution, were given some of the highest frequencies, we would be blown to dust. It would be like walking into the most powerful laser beam. Energies coming into this solar system are reduced in power by a being called the

Solar Logos, whom I will be talking more of later. The energies are also filtered again by combinations of stars and planets. One combination is made up of Polaris, the pole star, the constellation of the Great Bear, and another star, Vega, which make up a positive-neutral-negative triangle. This is being replaced by another combination, it would appear, and this is one reason for the shuffling of the stars indicated to Deborah.

We spent most of the rest of that day sleeping, until we were given the word to build the medicine wheel at Nose Hill just before midnight. Vehicles are not allowed on to the hill, and there is no natural way in by car anyway. But we had a pile of stones to take, so we had to find an entrance. The pendulum led us to a building site and a dirt track where the contractors' vehicles had their access. We reached a spot not far away from some houses on the edge of the hill, and we were told that this was the place and not, surprisingly, the old medicine wheel where we had been a few days earlier. It was a wet and misty night, and that provided the cover for what we had to do.

We had with us, according to instructions, all the diamond stones, many others which we had collected at the places we had visited, firewood, and some water. We arranged the diamond stones in a circle and built a base for a fire with the others. We walked the circle seven times to charge up the energy, and when the fire was lit and burning we had to ask the Great Spirit to help us to give power and Light to this sacred place. The other dimensions can't help unless we ask because that would be denying us free-will. This is why Christ said: "Ask and you shall receive". We had to sprinkle water on the fire as we said our words, which we had to repeat three times. Deborah said that about half way through this, crowds of Indian spirits came across the brow of the hill and stood watching us. With them were the spirits of a buffalo, deer, beaver, bear, eagle, butterfly, and a variety of birds and animals native to Canada.

As we left, the spirits began their work. No doubt this included ceremonies of forgiveness by all the souls who had contributed to the darkness that had blighted this crucial energy-point. The next day, as I caught my flight to the Animal Rights Conference in the United States, it was snowing and the weather was terrible. It stayed like that for the next four days, and no construction work was possible on the building site near the medicine wheel. It also took precisely that time for 1500 souls to take part in the ceremonies required to disperse the dark energies. When the cleansing was complete, this key point on the Earth's emotional body was working powerfully once again. This was crucial. The importance for all of us of stabilising the earth's emotions is beyond calculation.

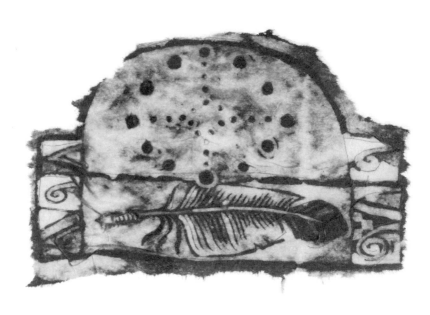

8

Journey to Aquarius

There was a time when a UFO sighting was a big event. Today there is an endless stream of reports and publications about people who have seen strange flying machines and 'aliens'. This is not surprising. There are many beings from other planets working to help the earth and its life-forms through the years ahead. These beings are not aliens, but our brothers and sisters in the divine family. They have become known as extra-terrestrials. In fact we are all extra-terrestrials when we are not in a physical body, but I am using this established term to describe those coming to us from other planets and star systems. A few are working with the forces of darkness, it is true, but the overwhelming majority are here to help us. They always come in numbers at critical times in our evolution, and the Bible contains descriptions of 'chariots' that are clearly spaceships, and talks of people arriving on beams of light.

There are many souls who have lived on earth over thousands of years who originate from other planets. I am one of them, and so are Linda and my children. We came from a planet called Oerael (pronounced Oreal) in another solar system, and arrived at the start of Atlantis. Most of those working to bring in the new age of Aquarius also came from other planets a long time ago.

To explain how and why this came about, and its significance for the future, we must look, briefly, at the history of the Earth and its fall from spiritual grace. The Godhead does not so much create as create the creators. I read at this time that solar systems are formed by deva spirits often known as archons. They produce the atomic structure of suns, around which new systems can come to revolve. Archons have a special ability to produce and manipulate matter to form asteroids, the so-called 'minor planets'. The archons create a swirling storm around the asteroids, made up of cosmic energy, minute particles of matter and other gases and substances. Over millions of years in our time-scale, the components of this cosmic dust-storm begin to cling to asteroids, and the asteroids cling to each other. As the mass spirals and spins, contracts and condenses, atomic-type reactions take place and a sun is formed. During this process, parts of the Sun break away and begin to rotate around it. These cool to become the planets and forms of the new solar system. That's what some of the books I came across at this time said, anyway. I await more information on this.

A sun is much more than a source of warmth. What we see from earth is only that part of our sun within our range of frequency. It has many non-physical aspects which go out across the whole of the solar system, and it sends to us certain spiritual vibrations. Our sun is a spiritual giant, and this is why the ancients used to worship it. They knew the sun's true significance. The avatar said of the sun:

She is the goddess of love and she will hold the answers... The heart, we know, is the centre of the emotional being and the pulse-point of our human membrane. The sun is the heart of our solar system, and she bleeds and burns and is outraged at earthlings for the destruction they have caused. The Sun's spiritual guide is the *Solar Logos*, that aspect of Godhead responsible for this solar system. Such mighty beings, and others, come into a new solar system after the archons have completed their work, and they supervise its development and the creation of life.

At this stage in the formation of the solar system other great beings from the deva kingdom start their work. The devas throw an etheric field or body around the new planet, and this field is programmed with the blueprint for the overall evolutionary design, the type of atmosphere and life-support systems required.

Under the direction of a planetary deva or archangel chemical changes are made which help to develop the first primitive life forms, and over massive periods of time these become vegetation and animals. Physical bodies are evolved by introducing to them higher and higher souls. It is the influence of the soul that changes the body until it reaches the perfection and standards of performance necessary for that period of the planet's evolution. It is important to remember that the evolution of the soul and the body are separate. The evolution of the body is only a process of developing a vehicle for the soul on any particular planet.

This solar system is much older than scientists have believed. They have estimated that the Earth was formed around 4,600 million years ago. According to communications from Rakorczy and others through Joan, the figure is more like 49,000 million! The Earth, we were told, suffered a catastrophe when energy from the sun pressed down on the atmosphere, contracting and condensing it, and destroying all organic matter. Evidence that science has gathered to make their estimate of 4,600 million years relates to the time when Earth began to recover from that disaster, not when the Earth was first created.

There was also a cataclysm which brought an end to the dinosaurs. This happened when another planet went across Earth's orbit, and their etheric bodies touched. Earth just survived, but it was fatal for the other planet's physical body, causing it to 'die'. Human life has also been here vastly longer than science has thought. Enormous evolution had already taken place before the first major civilisation emerged, called Mu, or Lemuria, as some people know it. China, Tibet and areas of the Middle East and South America were part of this land mass, in a world that looked very different from today.

The colossal and unexplained stone statues on Easter island, 2300 miles off the South American coast, were from Mu, which included the present Easter Island as part of its territory. The Mu-an civilisation survived, indeed flourished, for many thousands of years, and the more advanced of their number built the first cities. The remains of these can be seen several thousand feet up in parts of South America. They were lifted to that height by another cataclysm which brought Mu to a devastating conclusion. There have been many such geological changes through the life of Planet Earth, some a natural part of her evolution, some human-created. I feel that in Mu the latter was the case.

I believe that around the time we call Mu the effect of a misguided consciousness which became known as Lucifer began to be felt on the physical Earth. I think this aspect of consciousness made a challenge to the natural laws of Creation. By that I mean it opposed the principles of harmony, balance, and flow in the energies and harnessed the negative polarity for its own power. This caused fantastic disruption all over the Universe. The power of this consciousness gathered as it fed off the extreme negative energies it was creating and learned how to use them more and more destructively. Other aspects of consciousness were imbalanced and drawn into the web. The decision was made by those who wished to restore harmony, that this challenge had to be met. It is the deep memory of the Light-Dark struggle on other frequencies and in other areas of this frequency that has seeped into the conscious level of many science fiction writers to manifest itself as stories and films like 'Star Wars' and 'The Empire Strikes Back'.

The Luciferian Consciousness either caused havoc directly or worked through the minds and emotions of others. Planets were destroyed and there was devastation throughout this Solar System. The key planet Lucifer wished to control was the Earth because it is the heart chakra of at least this part of the Universe and the point from which the energy we call love emanates. I had a vision of the Earth as one of those glass balls you see hanging from the ceiling in dance halls and discos. Light was being beamed at the Earth and it was cascading and deflecting out from here to the Universe. This planet is also a point of balance. If you can unbalance, even destroy, the Earth then the effect on the Universe would be catastrophic, creating yet more negative energy and increasing the power of those feeding off it. This planet is, therefore, the scene of the ultimate spiritual showdown.

The Earth has been taken over by the Luciferian Consciousness. Aspects of it incarnated and others, in ever larger numbers, were controlled at the mind and emotional levels, by this consciousness while they were in incarnation. If you can scramble people mentally and emotionally you can make them lose contact with their higher selves and become servants of your will. This is the problem that humanity has faced from this period right up to the present day.

A call went out across the Universe and beyond for volunteers to come here and remove the Luciferian domination. The first incarnations of these volunteers from other planets came during the period of Mu and the biggest influx came at the start of the civilisation that followed Mu. This was Atlantis. These highly evolved beings created the most advanced and amazing civilisation the planet has yet seen. They used the power of crystals to create breathtaking cities of light and love. For a time Atlantis was paradise on Earth.

A communication from the Attarro Consciousness talked of how the Atlanteans worked with the dolphins. They were the animals beloved of the Atlantean era and communication was two-way. "They were the messengers and told of the currents and the weathers and of anyone who tried to enter this place of love and harmony. Dolphins were the epitome of true love and controlled the waters and the emotions. They taught the children to swim and to trust the waters."

In the beginning, the extra-terrestrials – the 'volunteers' – became the so-called High Priests of Atlantis. These were not High Priests in the religious sense, they were the keepers of the knowledge about the energies. They initiated others into these secrets, including Earth people, after a long and exhaustive series of teachings, tests and ceremonies. They were extremely careful about who had the knowledge; like everything, it could be used for good or ill. Knowledge is neutral. It is how you use it that is positive or negative and in the wrong hands the knowledge available in Atlantis was potentially catastrophic.

The Atlanteans understood how to use the natural laws to perform what we would call 'miracles.' They could manifest and demanifest things and move great objects by levitation. "Beam me up, Scotty" is not so far fetched as you may think, they could do that in Atlantis without any help from Scotty or anyone else. Their bodies were less dense and heavy than ours and they could do many things that we would find hard if not impossible to believe.

One communication from the Attarro Consciousness said that the Earth "...wept for the loss of her children (in the spiritual sense), for she remembered when Earthlings floated through tranquil skies and walked across her placid oceans. They communicated on all levels with the animals, plants, and rocks until the giant freeze vibration set in".

The 'freeze vibration' – dense matter – came when the harmony created by the early Atlanteans was destabilised by the Luciferian influence. Even most of those who had come to help the Earth were affected and they began to be controlled by the forces of disharmony and destruction. Mayhem was unfolding in the heavens as other planets were destabilised also. Some say this was the time the Moon fell into its present orbit around the Earth, causing colossal effects to this planet's energy fields. Once again Earth-shattering geological events unfolded and the map of the world was changed beyond recognition. There was an axis tilt and a tidal wave surged around the Earth. This was the 'Great Flood' mentioned in the Bible. The land mass called Atlantis disappeared and with it went the giant crystal at the heart of its power system. This crystal is still under the Atlantic Ocean and it is the effect of this which has created from time to time a gateway from this frequency to another. It is this that has led to the strange happenings in what is called the Bermuda Triangle.

The Earth was almost destroyed by the upheavals at the end of Atlantis, but just survived. Atlantis itself disappeared under the sea and it was this that allowed the Gulf Stream to flow northwards to warm the British Isles. Some of the background to this period was given to me in a channelling through a sensitive in the West of England. To 'channel' is to tune your consciousness to another frequency and allow information in the form of thought energy to be passed through your consciousness down to this level. Here your brain decodes the thought energy and turns it into spoken words. The communicator on this occasion gave the name Magnu:

> I feel you are sensing now the energies coming in, the energies surrounding your planet. This is causing many of you to ask questions. It is causing many of you to re-evaluate completely your way of life, where you feel you wish to go, what you want to do. It is causing tremendous upheavals. Some of these upheavals are very confusing, very distressing, very disturbing. Some people in relationships are finding they can no longer continue in those relationships because their partners cannot tune into what they are tuning into. It is causing a great deal of disturbance. And I have said to this sensitive on more than one occasion that you must organise yourselves into groups to support each other.

> Now then. My own allegiance with your planet goes back to an Atlantean period. At this time there were many energies being used and information and knowledge being used which were for particular reasons of safety withdrawn, shall we say, to prevent complete catastrophe, to prevent total destruction of your planet. One could say these were emergency measures if you like, to prevent the inhabitants of this planet from an untimely destruction.

> Now at that time, shall we say, this knowledge was distributed only to the few, it was taught in what one would call a temple setting, though I am very careful about using this word. It has connotations, maybe. So let me use that word in the broadest possible sense. There were those initiated into this knowledge. There were grades of initiation and those who passed the full initiation, these were known as Guardians of the Light and Keepers of the Secret Knowledge. This is the context from which I am coming.

> There came a time when this knowledge and the energies

were withdrawn. It is very difficult for me to explain to you precisely what I mean by that, so I will let you mull these things over. As the energies around your planet quicken, so these latent energies, these energies which have been withdrawn, will now be phased back in. They will gradually be awakened. As the consciousness level of the planet raises itself, those of you Light Workers who are working together to raise your consciousness, you will be able to hold more and more refined vibrations and so we will be able to use you as a catalyst to be able to feed in more and more energies.

As more of you raise yourselves to meet the challenge, so we can awaken more of these energies. Now, energy is consciousness and the energies themselves contain the knowledge and the information which is beginning to surface again in your consciousness, so that many of you will remember the Atlantean times. You will remember that you communicated with say, dolphins and whales. You understood these other sentient creatures. You could levitate. You could cause quite significantly large objects to levitate. You could manifest things. You could cause spontaneous combustion by not miraculous means at all. Once you know what you are doing these things follow. It is a matter of order.

Now I am looking to a time on your planet when these energies, this knowledge, is re-awakened and re-integrated into your consciousness. I am not looking to a time when this knowledge will be for a few, but when your whole planet will be awakened to this understanding which you have simply forgotten. It is not a matter of new information, it is a matter of remembering who you are and where you come from.

So you are being asked to change. You are being asked to change in a total way. It is not a matter of small changes, of a little thing here, a little thing there. You are really being asked to turn yourselves inside out. There is a massive shadow which must be cleared and it's up to Light Workers such as yourselves to focus yourselves on that challenge.

(I should say at this point that channellers decode the thought energy into language that reflects their own way of putting things. You will see what I mean here:)

> Those of you in the forefront of this, you are rather like a snowplough. You are the thin end of the wedge. You really have, how shall I put this? To a certain extent. I suppose, you have the shitty end of the job. You have got to do an awful lot, but nevertheless you are capable of doing an awful lot. That is why you have chosen to come, that is what you are here for, to really shovel some shit, and therefore make some space behind you to make it easier for the others.

The Magnu consciousness then asked for questions. I asked about the Earth's energy system. He confirmed what I said earlier about every life form having the system of chakras or power centres. We should imagine they were in sequences of seven, he said, although it was, in fact, not quite so simple as that. These power centres were like a fuse box. The fuse box in humans and the planet were not exactly the same, but they were similar.

> As in your human body, there are energy lines around your planet, through your planet, which correspond, I suppose, very much to the acupuncture lines and meridians in your body. Where two lines cross, you create a vortex (a whirlpool of energy), a tiny vortex if it's two. The more lines that intersect, the bigger the vortex. Therefore when you have a chakra you have a large vortex of intersecting energy. It is the same with your planet. Where the most lines cross, there is the biggest vortex. Now you could say the plexus (network) in and around the islands you call the British Isles is the hub of the wheel of plexuses and energies which surround your planet. It has acted in other times like a fail-safe device. In order to activate these chakric points upon your planet, the energies must all pass through the central point. They must pass through the heart of the pattern.

Magnu said the network had been created by previous Light

Workers over many thousands of years into ancient history. They had wanted to protect the energies and the planet, and they did this by creating a protective webbing, a protective shield around the World. This allowed the energies to be activated only by those who had access to the keys and knew what they were doing. When Magnu was incarnated on Earth in Atlantis, the Keepers of the Light had their individual 'keys'. Those who operated at the heart of the system had the greatest responsibility because they had the keys to all the systems as a fail-safe mechanism should anything go wrong. Once the centre of the pattern was shut down, all the other interconnecting systems around the planet were greatly limited also. "In effect" said Magnu "You switch it off." The keys, he said, were a "consciousness pattern, a series of harmonic equations, if you like, known only to the keepers of that pattern."

The British Isles was an important place to be, but he said we should not get too carried away by that. The energy system was interconnected, and every place depended on every other place to complete the circuit. At the end of Atlantis the keys were turned off in the British Isles to reduce the power of the energies so they could not be used to destroy the planet. They are now being turned back on and this is causing great changes on Earth as the old order crumbles in all its forms and the new begins to emerge.

Magnu talked of what happened when people worked with energy lines. The effect was two-fold. "When you start doing things to those lines, they start doing things to you." Yes, we were clearing blockages, but the work was also helping us to tune into the energy and the knowledge it carries. We were beginning to bring forth our memory, and it was important that the knowledge we carried within us from previous times was brought to the surface. This was the way it was to be done – not by him or other communicators, telling us everything. A crucial aspect of our experiences had been to activate our memories of the knowledge.

The effect of turning down the energies and the knowledge they carried was that we forgot what happened and what we learned in Atlantis and before. The higher the frequency of the energies around us, the higher levels of knowledge and intelligence we can tune into. In Atlantis those frequencies were much higher than they are today. When the energies were turned down our access to the Atlantean Consciousness was lost and so we 'forgot' it ever happened. In this way, the greatest civilisation this planet has seen is now looked upon as some sort of myth or fairy tale, a figment of the imagination. Gradually, those more powerful energies of the higher vibrations are being restored and this is will have – is having – a dramatic effect on all of us.

It is the role in this life for those re-incarnated Atlanteans to restore those energies. These are the beings from other planets and civilisations who came in to wrest control of the planet from the Luciferian Consciousness. As Magnu said:

> There are many of you for whom the Earth is not your indigenous evolutionary home, shall we say. There are many of you on this planet who come from other spheres of evolution. I think these have been called "star children" by some of your writers, that is a good enough expression. More evolved beings came to your planet and manifested on your planet in Atlantean times. This was the biggest impulse on bringing the new knowledge into Atlantis which caused it to grow into the civilisation that it was. New knowledge was brought into this system from universal sources from highly evolved spirits, bringing knowledge into the planet. And you're going to bring it back, basically.

With that, Magnu said goodbye and asked us to discuss together what we had heard. I should say that on these occasions the words we hear are less important than the thought forms we are absorbing on our other levels of being. It is a little like recording them on a video to be played later. The thought forms eventually filter through to the conscious level and appear as greater understanding and knowledge.

The sensitve could remember being with Magnu in Atlantis and the end of that civilisation around 10,500 BC. She could also remember what he and others looked liked in Atlantis, very different from our bodies today. They were much taller, around seven feet some of them, with a gold complexion and slanting, pale blue eyes. They had a more elongated skull and much higher hairline. They lived incredibly long physical lives, as did those in Mu. As this transformation continues, physical bodies on this planet will again look every different and will live for hundreds of years.

The sensitive is also one of the extra-terrestrials who helped to build Atlantis. She believes she went astray after that glorious beginning. Today those volunteers from other planets who survived the onslaught of the Luciferian Consciousness through the period since then are few compared with the population of the planet. They are the ones who have come through so many tests to show that they are capable of being trusted to do the work in this incarnation when the Luciferian control is being removed.

It is these souls who have carried the knowledge through the centuries since Atlantis in civilisations and communities like the early Egyptians, the Essenes, the early Incas, the Cathars, the native American Indians, and others. The most famous of these volunteers from other realms was the man we call Jesus. In this Gateway edition of the Truth Vibrations I have made a few changes to the original text for two reasons: (a) I feel the themes of it are correct although my understanding (memory) of the detail is evolving all the time and (b) this book was written at the start of my conscious awakening and it will be interesting for people to read my later books to see how the process of awakening and understanding unfolds and develops. However, I feel it is worth inserting here what I feel is the basic truth about Jesus as it has evolved in my consciousness between the first edition written in 1990 and this one published in the closing weeks of 1993.

The following information I channelled directly through myself and I was amazed to see how it is supported by others who have either channelled the same or come to this conclusion from historical research:

Jeshua (Jesus is a translation from the Jewish) was born in the normal way and not by some virgin miracle. It was his task to stand up and speak out for the truth and challenge the Luciferian-controlled status quo. He was linked closely with the Essene Community which lived alongside the Dead Sea at

Qumran where the Dead Sea Scrolls were found after the Second World War. In his early life he travelled widely to places like India, learning from those he met or, more to the point, remembering what he already knew, but had forgotten in the process of incarnation into a dense physical body. He was also a channel for bringing immensely powerful healing and transforming energies to the Earth, energies that have become known as the Christ. This is the energy of pure love. The vibratory rate of his energy field was so high that he could channel energies of a power that would have fried most people on Earth at that time. So his task was to pass on information that would help to open the minds of people to who they really are, and to channel energies into this physical frequency that would help to re-balance the planet and in this way also trigger and awaken people as they became less affected by Luciferian domination.

This was not an attempt to remove the Lucifer Consciousness completely. It would not have been possible then and the time for that was planned well in advance to be the period we are living through today. This is why so many prophecies by Nostradamus, Edgar Cayce, the Hopi Indians and many others, point to now for the time of great change. What Jesus and those working with him were here to do was channel enough energy, remove enough negativity, and change the collective consciousness enough for the planet to be able to survive until now. This they clearly achieved.

Far from being the celibate he is claimed to be by the Church. I believe Jesus fathered at least three children by at least two women. The one known as Mary Magdalene was his main life partner, possibly his wife. His task was enormously difficult, especially since those who incarnated with him also affected the imbalances of the planet and the limitations of perception within the dense physical form. In the end so many people turned against him that he was nailed to a cross to silence him. But I do not believe that he died there. I feel that the man called Joseph of Arimathea was his natural father and that he had enough influence and money to ensure that Jesus was taken from the cross alive, though in a desperate condition. My own feeling, and what I have channelled and 'seen', leads me to believe strongly that he survived. I had a very strong vision of Jesus on the cross. During that vision I was with Jesus, experiencing what he felt. He experienced great pain in his hands and wrists, and he was utterly exhausted. I then saw a pole being raised with a cloth which was offered to his mouth. From this he took a drink. Soon after this he appeared to lose consciousness. When he awoke he was lying with people all around him, attending to his wounds. They were all in white, I remember. It was clear that Jesus was in a state of shock. He whispered "I live, I live", as though he had expected to have left the physical body. I had other visions and channelling, which together gave me this overall picture of what actually happened two thousand years ago.

Joseph of Arimathea had persuaded the authorities to have the crucifixion on his land – the Garden of Gethsemane. Joseph was a rich man and not without influence. The Authorities did not realise that he was Jesus's real father. When Jesus was offered a wet rag on the end of a pole to give him a drink, it contained a drug that brought about the appearance of death.[2] Joseph of Arimathea organised this, no doubt with a bribe here and there, and the 'dead' body was taken away to the Essene Community where Jesus recovered after a long convalescence. Very few people knew what was happening and even Mary, his mother, and Mary Magdalene were not in on the plot. They believed he had died until they were later re-united with him.

Jesus, I believe, lived a long life and visited many countries, including Britain, passing on information and channelling energies, but none of this was recorded by history. In the eyes of the historians and the people of Jerusalem and the Roman Empire, he died on the cross. I feel that had he and others not channelled vast amounts of healing energy at that time, the Earth could well have been out of existence by now. All through this period since Atlantis those other groups I have mentioned have come to work on the energy system and human consciousness to keep the Earth alive until today and the time of the Great Cleansing. I have no doubt that the consciousness that we call Jesus is back in incarnation now to play a part in this. All that knowledge and experience would not be wasted at this of all times. And the last people to recognise him will be the churches who claim to worship him. Indeed they will laugh at him or condemn him as a blasphemer and imposter!

This time his words will not be perverted as they have largely been in the Church under the influence of the Luciferian Consciousness. The Church in its many forms has caused wars to be fought over dogmas that it created and has fostered fear and terror of some mythical, vengeful God. So much blood has been shed in the name of a being who was the very expression of love and peace for all.

The Lucifer influence is responsible for much of this, but it would be misguided for humanity to blame everything on that source of imbalance. It can only succeed in manipulating our minds and values if we allow it to and for so long humanity has given in. It is time to make a stand. This is one reason why the extra-terrestrials are encircling the Earth in larger and larger numbers, to help us to defeat these forces and make a gigantic leap in evolution into the Aquarian Age when humankind, or those who are evolved enough to meet the challenge, will rise out of the abyss of misunderstanding at last. They are here to guide us through tremendously difficult times with love, wisdom, and understanding. For let us not deceive ourselves about the momentous task it will be to lead humanity through some turbulent years and back into the Light where we belong.

The highest levels of Divine Consciousness are now standing together as One to guide this planet into the new age of balance and enlightenment. We are now being offered the opportunity to be part of a new world and new Earth based on love and harmony. What greater gift, what greater challenge, could we be given? What greater vision could be put before us?

9

New Vibrations

After seven months of intensive spiritual education and guidance from some very highly-evolved beings, I now understand something of the changes the earth and ourselves are going through, but there is still an enormous amount that I still do not know. It is also clearer to me why these books are being written and what they are intended to achieve. With every book my consciousness, my ability to understand what is happening and why, will be opened wider, as will my eternal memory. This is, apparently, deliberate. They could have contacted me years ago and taken me much further along the remembering process before I was launched into print. They didn't because that is not the way they have chosen to bring the message before the world. Each successive book will be more detailed and go deeper into the creation and evolution of life and the transition we are going through.

I have no doubts whatsoever that some of what I have said in terms of detail I will modify in future books. That is unavoidable in the circumstances in which I am working. The idea is for the readers to grow with me as my knowledge and understanding is increased at each stage of the programme agreed and set out before I incarnated.

I have offered to you what I was asked to produce, a basic explanation of the universe and the imminent transformation of life on earth. I am in the privileged position of being guided out of the mist, and these books are designed to take others with me. There is a phenomenal way to go and there is much we will never know within the confines of a physical body. Even Jesus had problems coping with its limitations as he went in search of the Truths. There is always the frustration of seeing one new fact demand six new questions, but many truths are within our grasp. I have outlined some of them here, such as reincarnation, karma, and the energy-system.

I should however add some notes of caution at this stage. Communication between other planes and dimensions and ourselves is not like picking up the telephone The thought-forms have to be processed by the physical brain, and in so doing some of the sharpness of the message can be lost – not the general meaning, but the fine detail can get distorted. It doesn't mean the detail is necessarily less than accurate, but it can be. Different spirit communicators may also have their own interpretation and emphasis. There are many communications I have not included because they have yet to be confirmed by other independent sources. Where I have used messages of this kind, I have said so. It should also be remembered what I said earlier about the difficulties the other realms have sometimes in judging our time, and the time-scales are often changing anyway in response to human behaviour. You should bear that in mind when I give dates. They are the latest dates I have at the time of writing in November 1990. The only thing we can be certain about is that we are talking about this decade and we should concern ourselves more with the consistent themes than with the fine detail.

Having stressed those points I can say with great confidence that, at the very least, the vast majority of what you have read and are about to read is absolutely correct. With that, let us conclude this first stage of the story.

The evolution of the earth is arranged into ages, identified by the astrological symbols. Jesus came to herald the age of Pisces, and we are now entering the age of Aquarius. This is when we are to learn the oneness of everything. We will see that all life-forms, animals, plants, minerals, devas, humans and planets, are created by the same source with the same energy. We are all on a magical journey of evolution back to the God-head. We are all part of one another. We are all the same one consciousness at different stages of evolution.

We knew this once long ago, but our spiritual standards declined, and the power that built the glory of Atlantis was switched off to stop the planet being blown apart. A group of Atlanteans who had retained their purity and values came to Britain, the hub of the energy-system, to shut down the power-ful energies. They based themselves in Cornwall, and one At-lantean used his special energy-pattern and knowledge to switch off these powerful energies. At the same time in South America, a people who were eventually to become the Incas were chan-nelling a lower energy into the earth to replace it. Other people were also involved in different parts of the world.

But who was this mighty Atlantean who came to Britain? It might help if I said the symbol for the energies he was working with is the sword. The Atlantean was the man the legends call King Arthur, and with him was Merlin. The story of the sword Excalibur was symbolic of those energies being switched off. The Holy Grail is not an object, but levels of consciousness and spiritual awareness. That is what the Knights of the Round Table were searching for in what has become known as the pursuit of the Holy Grail. Anything that helps to develop this understanding, this state of being, could fairly be linked to the Holy Grail.

When humanity showed that we were not yet evolved enough to be trusted with the higher energies, we had to begin a series of lessons before we qualified for another chance. These lessons have taken the form of learning the right way, or at least seeking it, by experiencing the wrong one. The Lords of the Rays such as Rakorczy look after twelve rays of energy, seven of which affect us directly while we are in a physical body. A mixture of these seven is given to each of us when we incarnate to set us challenges and tests and give us the opportunity to learn the lessons we have chosen for ourselves. Another separate combination is given to the Earth-spirit.

These rays are: ray one – pure will and power; ray two –

love and wisdom; ray three – intelligence (rational intellect, not wisdom); ray four – harmony through conflict; ray five – concrete mind and science; ray six – love and devotion; ray seven – law and order and ceremonial magic, the Rakorczy ray.

Our personal mixture sets us individual lessons, while the Earth mixture sets the curriculum for the Earth-spirit and humanity as a whole. In the age just passing, the main energies have been numbers three (intelligence), four (harmony through conflict) and five (concrete mind and science). How long we took to learn the lessons they set was our choice. We could have made it easy for ourselves, or very difficult. For instance, you can learn through wisdom that it is better to seek harmony rather than conflict, or you can learn it by experiencing two World Wars. This doesn't mean we were made to fight wars – nothing is more abhorrent to the spiritual Masters. It was our choice.

It has been the same with human science. We could have seen a long time ago that you cannot explain the great mysteries of life through merely mechanical means, but we didn't. Now with science hitting countless dead-ends in its attempt to explain those mysteries, more and more people are looking for spiritual answers. Another example is the material society. Again, we could have seen before now that judging our own success and that of our countries by how much we consume was bound to destroy the Earth and all life upon it. Instead we have had to learn the hard way by experiencing what materialism is doing to great tracts of the planet.

When you look from the wider perspective of evolution, however, that is not necessarily a bad thing as long as we don't go too far. The hardest lessons are the best learned. You can see this in the numbers of people who have become disillusioned with the present way of life and are looking for new meaning. This makes them fertile ground for the spiritual truths that are now being offered to them. The present energy combination is being joined by ray seven, law and order and ceremonial magic. This will help us to raise our spiritual understanding and bring order from chaos. This is what the voice communication meant when it said: "The three will be replaced by four. The three points of the triangle will become the four points of the diamond. Another kind of energy is being added that will transform life on earth". We are already seeing that transformation in action and, as they say, 'we ain't see nothin' yet'.

As people have tuned to the new vibrations, we have had the rise of the Green movement, anti-cruelty movements, and vegetarianism. We have begun to care for the Earth and see other forms of life as fellow expressions of Creation and not as commodities to be made as fat as possible as quickly as possible and sold for as much as possible. The meat industry is seeing these new values on the balance sheet, and as the vibrations speed up, businesses based on cruelty or the exploitation of animals, people or the Earth, will be in serious trouble.

The division in our societies between those who are tuning in and those who are not is becoming more evident with every year. It is the division between those looking for a new direction, a new path, and those still stuck in the delusions of materialism. These divisions are breaking up relationships of all kinds, as partners and colleagues begin to view life with a difference of perspective that is soon to become a chasm. Humanity is being divided into those racing forward spiritually and those still holding on to yesterday. It is the former group that will bring about the 'cultural revolution' that Wang predicted for Britain by 1995. It will be the same in every country at some time in the next ten years, and you can see that the potential for conflict and confrontation between the two groups is enormous during this changeover period. The responsibility lies with those tuning in to avoid this through peace, love and understanding at all times.

Imagine what all this will do to the world economy, the system of destruction, as hundreds of millions reject the belief that consumption is the meaning of life and the measurement of our success and well-being. The idea that economics should be based on setting people against people and country against country in brutal competition will be just as soundly rejected, as will the exploitation of the weak by the powerful. Anyone tuned to the new vibrations could not live with such injustice.

This, along with the economic implications of geological upheavals, extreme weather events, and military conflict, will see the world financial system collapse. This was inevitable at some stage anyway because it is built on self-delusion, but it will be hastened. We will have to create barter economies, goods and services being exchanged for other goods and services on a local or regional level. The orgy of materialism in the latter period of the Pisces age is taking its final bow. The planet cannot take the punishment and so the system is being removed.

A message from Attarro in October 1990 predicted serious economic difficulties. "Estimated economic flows will change drastically and the economic system will need much attention as the currency falls flat on its face. Disaster after disaster, you say. It is not necessarily disaster, it is an opening for new opportunity in learning on many levels. The peoples sometimes have to be shaken up to open their eyes and their new awareness".

The spirit realms are doing all they can to avoid conflict and wars breaking out amid the chaos and confusion, not least because the thought-energy that would be generated by wars would be extremely harmful to the Earth and the energy-system, especially at this critical time. But they can do only so much to influence us. Human free will can always override them if we choose to allow darkness to reign. It needs us all to meditate and visualise peace. The economic, human, weather and environmental pressures will bring with them tremendous political changes, too, and from what I gather very few of the big political names in the world today will stay in office, or opposition, as the vibrations accelerate in the 90s. A message through the Kenilworth source on September 8th 1990 said that Margaret Thatcher would not be Prime Minister of Britain for very much longer:

> You have a woman who speaks with too loud a voice and cannot feel the tempo of the seasons. She will go before the changes come and the ones who will rule are prepared for the work they must undertake. Fear not. It is not our way to bring pain to humankind, but decisions have to be made in which we play our part.

On November 3rd, ten days before the Deputy Prime Minister, Sir Geoffrey Howe, resigned, came this: "There are already changes within your government and others will follow swiftly. It will be necessary for a different style of government to be established". Two weeks later Mrs Thatcher was forced to resign. She will not be the only political casualty as the new spiritual climate increasingly turns us away from the responses of anger and aggression and replaces them with love and peace. The automatic writing said that the politicians had not been taught the ways of the ancients or they feared a power greater than their own. They fought with weapons and anger to preserve what was theirs when the universe really belonged to everyone and could not be divided in this way. Everything was for the good of all and should be shared equally across many lands.

The world political scene will change on a scale and often with the speed of what we saw in Eastern Europe, which was, itself, a manifestation of the new vibrations at work. I was told by one message from Rakorczy of changes in the Soviet Union, with Mr Gorbachev replaced as president before 1992. This would lead to the states of the USSR being self-governed. They would operate as independent countries within an overall organisation that would co-ordinate co-operation between them. This would set the example which the rest of the world would eventually follow.

The present way of life in the United States was also coming to an end before the end of the decade, according to a Kenilworth communication: "On the other side of your large ocean, there will be many changes in government. This part of your world has for too long sought happiness through greed and has given little thought to the needs of other people. In particular, they have not concerned themselves sufficiently with the knowledge their brown brothers carry".

Every other nation would go through political and economic transformation, although in Britain the Establishment were likely to cling to the old illusions longer than most, said the spirit guides. A new political grouping would emerge in Britain made up of Greens and others who had seen the Light. The Green Party, I was told, should be developing policies for a time of economic collapse, and these should include plans for barter economies based on local communities. The reference to 'those who will rule' after the present order has gone were souls who had incarnated for this purpose, although most did not yet realise that. A piece of automatic writing to the sensitive in Northamptonshire spoke of "One with unearthly experience", who would appear early in the next century, to "hold the hand of humanity".

We can expect to see people acting strangely and behaving completely out of character. This is the result of them tuning to the new vibrations and seeing life differently, or struggling to tune in and becoming confused, bewildered and disorientated. We are likely to see this manifest in gathering conflict around the world. There will be health effects, too, with diseases such as AIDS rampant, particularly in Africa, by 1993. New diseases will emerge and others will fade as the energies change. People's health and behaviour will make it very clear who is tuning in and who is not, and we must give all the help and support we can to those who are finding it difficult. All the old certainties and stabilities will disappear in the changeover period, and getting ourselves together in groups to support each other is vital. Children are the ones who will adapt best because most of their souls will have incarnated specifically for the new age and they will find it easier to follow the quickening vibrations.

As the vibrations speed up, so does time as we measure it. When people say, "there are not enough hours in the day to do everything anymore", they are right. It is important we recognise this and stop trying to do all we have done in the past. We must simplify our lives. If we don't, we will burn ourselves out mentally and physically because, unknown to us, the days are getting shorter and will continue to do so. I was warned by the Avatar that I would find that time passed incredibly quickly, perhaps frighteningly so, and this was a reference to the phenomena I have described.

The great institutions in our modern societies will fall, including the British monachy and the traditional churches in their present form. They will only survive at all if they adapt their thinking radically and immediately to encompass the spiritual truths of reincarnation and karma which are about to return to Western spiritual life after their years in the wilderness. The new spirituality involves a one-to-one relationship with the Godhead and the higher intelligences. We will no longer believe that all our sins can be forgiven by a priest appointed by the

Church hierarchy. Why do we need a human to arbitrate between ourselves and God when we have our own personal link? We should still meet together for our spiritual ceremonies because numbers add to the power, but it will be very different to what we see today. The traditional Churches will crumble.

All life-forms will be affected by the new vibrations and geological events. Some are likely to become extinct as their habitats change. A communication to Deborah Shaw in Canada said the African elephant, the blue whale, the osprey and the panda will not be with us beyond the end of the decade. Their species are going out of evolution and their souls will return in other species. There will be new ones emerging with the new frequencies, and it will be the same with the plant kingdom. But it has been stressed that we must protect the dolphin, which is the most highly evolved of the earth's animal and marine life. The dolphins are the last link with the sound system of Atlantis, and if they disappear it is going to be much more difficult for us to learn how to communicate with the animals. Research into dolphins and their sounds hold the key to this understanding. It is hard to believe, but true, that there was a time on Earth when animals did not attack humans. We were friends. It was only when we lost the sense of oneness that fear of humans brought the divisions between us.

It is impossible to say exactly what the geological impact will be because the forecasts are constantly changing as humankind wields its collective free will. What is certain is that we will have earthquakes and volcanoes of a power beyond modern human experience along with breathtaking weather extremes. It is also certain that this is all linked to the individual and collective karma of humanity, and we can work through that karma by turning to the Light or by experiencing tough lessons of our own creation. It would appear, at the time of writing, that we are in for an axis shift and a shift of both the magnetic and physical poles. This would seem to be supported in Revelations, the last book of the Bible. Revelations is not about one period but the evolution of humankind, and I know that we are approaching the point when the sixth seal will be opened:

And I saw the Lamb break open the sixth seal. There was a

violent earthquake and the sun became black like coarse black cloth and the moon turned completely red like blood. The stars fell down to the earth, like unripe figs falling from the tree when a strong wind shakes it. The sky disappeared like a scroll being rolled up and every mountain and island was moved from its place.

That would appear to be a description of how an axis shift would look and feel to those on earth at the time.

A session with Rakorczy and members of his team, communicating through Joan in Wales, gave us an explanation of at least part of what is happening. Everything has positive-negative polarities. Planets go through periods when they are positive or negative in their relationships with other planets. Each one is linked to another of an opposite polarity, and as their energies pass between them they try to find the balance between the two. The earth has been going through a positive stage, and the negative balance has come from a planet called Constabor in another solar system – this link with Constabor was also given independently to another source. Every time you move up to another level of evolution, the poles switch around. The Earth is changing polarities and Constabor is doing the same. It is this, we were told, that will bring about the shift in the magnetic poles and, as a consequence, the axis tilt.

As with the human body, the changes in the physical Earth come some time after the changes in the organising blueprint of the etheric body. Rakorczy and his team said the pole shift and axis tilt would happen in the etheric blueprint in Autumn 1994 or, if we help the Earth between now and then, Autumn 1995. The later date would be better because it would cause less damage. This, in turn, would lead to a pole shift and axis tilt on the physical body, the one we see and live on, in either 1998 or 1999. It was due to be an axis movement of 10%, but, thanks to the recent improvement in human thought-patterns, it is now due to be 5%.

The messages said the Earth's core was changing its composition. It is currently a liquid crystal with energy-particles of iron. This creates the planet's electromagnetic field and gives the earth her positive polarity in the relationship with Constabor.

The iron is gradually being replaced by the energy-particles of berkelium[3], which would give the Earth a negative polarity. This would enhance her female, receptive, spiritual aspects and it would have a similar effect on us also. Part of the phasing-in process involves the use of radioactive radon gas in the core, and you may know that radon gas has been causing problems in some areas. This will increase in the transition period.

The Earth wobbles on her axis and this, we were told, was the result of the Earth-spirit not being able to control and balance the conflicting forces around her. The time would come when the Earth would have no wobble, she would spin on a perfect upright axis. Now whether all that came across the frequencies in exactly the form it was sent we shall have to wait and see, but the general theme is beyond doubt.

There will be massive earth movements, volcanoes and great extremes of weather. As things currently stand, we can expect to see signs of this by 1992, and particularly during 1993-94. This cleansing will also lead to many apparently inexplicable fires at sacred sites and key power-centres around the world, to remove sources of imbalance. There was specific mention of one major fire we can expect in the north of England, the 'Kingdom of the Brigantes', though this one will not necessarily be on sacred ground: "There will be a great fire which will last for many days, and many will be needed from other parts of the world to bring it under control".

Every solstice from now on will see the pace of change quicken in its effect on all forms of life. The axis and pole shifts will cause fantastic winds in the days it will take for stability to return and there will be more earth movements and eruptions to relieve the pressure as everything re-tunes to the new regime. Sea rises, like the winds, have been mentioned many times in communications. They will take the form, in part, of tidal waves caused by the axis tilt, the pole shift, and the earth movements.

I was led to a book which explained the background to earthquake- and volcano-induced tidal waves. In some parts of the world the water table has been lowered while pollution has been cleared and the earth cured of what was described as a sort of leukaemia, cancer of the blood, or, in this case, of the water channels which carry the energy. This will mean that in some regions there will be a lot of rain and flooding as the water is returned while in others, said a communication to the Northamptonshire source, "there will be new areas of drought as the Earth empties her deepest caverns to prepare for the new flows of energy". Messages have said that the damage from all these events would appear to be random, but in fact it would relate to the karma of a country or region in terms of its treatment of the planet and all forms of life. For instance, we should expect to see those areas involved in taking oil to be prevented from doing so. This god of the material world is a vital lubricant which the Earth must have, and too much has been taken already by our insatiable system. The oil business will soon be history.

Precisely how the world will change, how quickly and on what scale, is still not known and, I repeat, the exact details and timings are subject to revision depending on how we react. But change there will be, and of a kind we could not begin to comprehend as we look around us today.

Whoever we are and whatever we are, the quickening vibrations of Aquarius cannot be ignored.

10

The Message

The great souls we have been working with have made it clear many times that there is a tremendous amount we can do to help ourselves and the planet through this period and reduce, perhaps dramatically, the scale and impact of the geological events.

The first thing we must do is avoid self-condemnation or the condemnation of those we perceive to be most responsible for guiding us down the wrong path. Most of them did not mislead us through malice, but because they, themselves, were misled. Over many lives we are all responsible for the misunderstandings and lost spiritual truths of reincarnation, karma, the energy-system, and a non-judgmental God. We should be seeking solutions, not scapegoats.

The way forward is, as ever, through love, peace and forgiveness. Unconditional love, unconditional peace, unconditional forgiveness. And the first step to forgiving others is to forgive ourselves, to love ourselves, and to make peace with ourselves. Guilt is a destructive emotion and we should be rid of it before we go any further. We know we have done wrong, but we must not live in the past or even in the future, but the present, the Now. This is the first day of the rest of our eternity. As the Avatar said:

Man should not experience guilt. He needs to acknowledge wrong and put things right where he can. He should ask for forgiveness and forgive himself. Guilt is man-made to stop man reaching his spiritual potential. This has developed since the crumbling of Atlantis and all ancient civilisations. This germ has taken hold and we must eliminate that germ of guilt. How can we love the Earth and our people? We love ourselves.

This kind of love is rather deeper than standing in front of a mirror admiring the reflection. It is not, either, to ignore the things we and others do. It is to love ourselves unconditionally; to accept that we are not perfect, and while we always search for perfection, we know that we will often fall short of what we might desire; it is to rid ourselves of our guilt, fears and insecurities, which shield us from our real selves, that spark of Light deep within us that knows who we really are. Let that Light shine and radiate through us and the darkness shall fade away. If we can do that the darkness shall lift from the Earth, also.

If we want to change the world, we have to change ourselves. It is our own guilt, fear and dislike of ourselves that makes us attack others for displaying the very faults that we wish we could banish from our own personalities. Once we are at peace with ourselves and love ourselves for what we are, imperfections and all, we will be in a position to love others with their imperfections. This is important, not only for the harmony of the human race, but also for the Earth as she goes through her traumatic transition.

One message from Rakorczy summed up the main problem for the Earth: "She is feeling unloved". She is not alone in that. All of humanity is feeling unloved, and so are the animals, the plants, and the rocks, as they have been exploited in the chase for the mythical utopia called 'economic expansion'. The dark energy-forms that our aggression, anger, fear and resentment have created are the most destructive contribution we have made to the planet's decline. It follows that the best way we can help the Earth-spirit through this period is to replace the darkness with Light. Hence, love, peace and forgiveness must prevail.

The law of like-attracts-like means that dark energy-forms attract others of the same kind, and this can create a massive cloud of darkness. It is a sort of spiritual magnetism at work. People can find themselves tapping into those dark energy clouds and having their attitudes and behaviour affected as a consequence. This is how dictators like Hitler can assemble nations behind their creed of hatred. The minds of people tune to these fields of darkness, and the more they do, and the more their own thoughts are affected, the bigger the cloud becomes. This leads to war and conflict, and leaves the Earth's energy system in ruins.

But Light also attracts Light, and that is the way we can shield the Earth from the darkness and give her the strength to go through her changes with the least possible turmoil. The Earth is a living being, with feelings and emotions and, as many communications have said, she is struggling to cope with the pressure. Imagine how we would be feeling if we were going through such a transition while physically and mentally drained, and with our blood supply diminished. Don't let anyone tell you that the Earth does not feel all the pain and anguish of what has been done to her.

Communications from Rakorczy and others have said that the strange weather patterns we have experienced in every part of the world are the result of the Earth-spirit suffering the effects of, particularly, emotional pressures. She is becoming confused. This is making her lose control, and the natural order of the planet is failing. As with the human form, upsets in the mental and emotional bodies disrupt the etheric organisation, and so affect the physical. We have had some highly destructive winds in Britain and Europe in recent years, and we can expect the power and frequency of hurricanes to increase. A message said there would be a severe hurricane around the Gulf of Mexico and New Orleans. Automatic writing to the Kenilworth source contained further warnings:

You must tell your friends on the other side of the world (New Zealand) that their small homes must be protected against wind, as the storms will gather around their islands and do great damage. In many other places the waters have begun to lift and much land will soon be no more. Not enough work has been done to protect your big city (London), and there will be many who are blamed and will lose their responsibilities as a result. In the East (of the world) the floods will soon begin and the storms will rage across the southern ocean. In the north the land becomes very cold as the winter snow and ice covers the ground. Here there will be many problems with food delivery and transport and many countries will be asked to help, or people will starve.

In the south (of Britain), the rains will fall heavily and inundate many areas... The east of your country will be very badly affected, and much of your fertile land will disappear...

In the north, strong winds will be the greatest hazard and, in particular, large amounts of snow will fall and lie on the ground for many months.

Your transport system will be badly affected and it will be necessary for everyone to store up their food supplies, as the power circuits will not operate for some time.

In the west, there will be large amounts of rain and snow, and the sea will rise and cover a considerable area.

These communications were received in October and November 1990. I must stress, again, however, that how bad they are, or even if some of them come to pass at all, depends on how we conduct ourselves. What we can say is that, as things currently stand, the world will be faced with severe and, in modern times, unprecedented weather conditions, and these will be caused by the mental and emotional turmoil the Earth-spirit is going through and the energy changes around the planet as the vibrations quicken. You can see why so many of us are being asked to work on the Earth's mind and emotions. If they can be settled down, it will be better for everyone. The scale of the damage of all types depends to a significant extent on the Earth-spirit's ability to maintain control under enormous pressure.

The series of messages which explained the changes in the

core also emphasised the importance of the Earth's emotional health. The shock of the axis and pole shifts would, we were told, cause the Earth-spirit to lose consciousness for one or two days, and daylight would disappear from the planet for that period. Light is also an energy-frequency and would be affected when the Earth-spirit goes into her short coma. When she regained consciousness, the messages said, she would be confused and bewildered, and order would take some time to return. All these things could be eased if humans were determined enough and far-sighted enough to help the Earth-spirit now.

I have heard some people offer the opinion that there is nothing we can do. It is all pre-ordained, they say. But that is overwhelmingly not the case with the communications I have seen and heard. Quite the opposite, in fact. We can give the Earth emotional and physical strength if we spend a few minutes every day sending her love and Light. All you have to do is visualise the Earth-spirit in any way you feel right, and imagine a stream of bright Light and love pouring down to her. See the darkness around her lifting away, leaving her surrounded with pulsating white or golden Light. It is important, nay crucial, I am told, for us to send the Light to the centre, the spiritual heart of the earth.

Much love-energy has been spread on the surface of the planet as a result of the Green movement and concern for the environment since the mid-eighties. This is wonderful and necessary, but it is the Earth-spirit, or the *Dynos* as some prefer to call her, which is in most desperate need of love and Light. I know all of this might sound ridiculous to some people, probably the majority at the moment, but I hope that many will begin to appreciate how thoughts create the very events they visualise. It happens instantly on the non-physical planes, and eventually on the physical. It is even better if you can get your friends to do it with you. Hold hands in a ring, and the power of your thought-energy will be much increased. I would urge that everyone organising any event large or small should include a few minutes at the beginning or end to go through the ceremony of sending love and Light to the Earth.

Under spiritual guidance there are groups of people

throughout the world who are building a network of Light, sending out love and peace to the Earth, her people, and all her creatures. Among them is Fountain International, which is based in Britain[4]. Join them and help them to build a network of Light that no darkness can breach. Just be careful, though, of what organisations you get involved with. Check them out. Not everything that calls itself 'New Age' is desirable. Some of it is not. Walking around in a spiritual daze and ignoring the practical necessities of life on a physical plane is of little use to anyone. It is balance we are searching for.

Visualise the shields of darkness lifting from the energy-lines around and through the earth. See the Light flowing unchallenged through the ley-lines and the whole planet glowing with brilliant Light. Send Light and love to the animals, the plants, the devas, and the rocks. Send it to anyone and any place that might be surrounded by the emotions of darkness. This is particularly needed, for example, in war zones and at meat and poultry factories, slaughterhouses, factory farms, and other buildings and sites where there is fear and suffering. Visualise such places, and those who work and fight in them glowing with the Light of love. We will change their attitudes far more quickly and effectively this way than by hurling abuse at them. It is the same with those who work in animal experimental laboratories.

This is something I hope that all campaigners and groups will come to accept soon. Many already have. Even when we are trying to stop bad things happening, we should not meet anger with anger or hatred with hatred. All you get that way is double the anger, double the hatred, and a bigger cloud of darkness. This is just what the darkness wants. Darkness can't cope with Light, darkness prefers more darkness. So we must meet aggression and hate with peace and love in large enough amounts, if the Light is to triumph.

I was guided into and out of the 'angry young man' stage myself in this life to show me it didn't work and make me receptive to these truths. I have known of people who have changed their attitudes when, unknown to them, someone has been sending them thought-forms of love. The best way to change aggressors and dictators is not by war and bitterness. It is through visualising these people and their countries bathed in the Light of love. If enough of us do this, we can disperse the dark energies they are tuning into, and their outlook on life will change. They won't be able to help themselves, for their source of darkness will have gone. I know that many people have been doing this for the countries of Eastern Europe for many years. This must be stepped up massively from now on whenever there is conflict, anger and hatred. The dark forces are working through all potential aggressors and often through those who oppose their aggression, too, to bring about war.

The next step for the Green Movement is to encompass this spiritual dimension more completely. If the pressure groups take the purely physical approach based on the limitations of current scientific thinking, they will be telling only half the story. The key threat to the Earth will go on being ignored. It is time, I would suggest, that the movement turned its collective mind to the Earth's energy-system, and sought protection for power centres, ley-lines and sacred sites.

Everything we need to do to help the Earth and ourselves comes down to love, peace and forgiveness. Whatever the mixture of the seven rays we receive on earth, they can always be balanced by ray two, love and wisdom. If we tune to this ray we automatically receive the best aspects, and avoid the worst, of all the others. This happens as a matter of course once we allow love, peace, forgiveness, tolerance, understanding, sharing, caring, and respect for others to dominate our values. The Avatar put it like this:

> Send out love through thoughts and acts, write down words of love, eliminate violence of any level, whether mental, physical or emotional. Gentleness within the temple of our soul needs to shine through the windows of our eyes... There is much divine joy around us, and beauty of inexplicable abundance, if we can lift our faces upwards and let the Light of God shine upon us.

And as this book was being completed a message was channelled through Deborah Shaw in Canada, which emphasised the power of love and the meaning of life:

Every wave that breaks upon the shore, every drop of rain, every puff of wind, is all part of the Creator's Plan and contributes to life. Karma is not about recriminations, it is our opportunity to learn to love, expand, learn, and love again.

If people suffer physically as a result of what is to come, that is part of their karma. We need, each one of us, to look inwards and learn to accept what is being offered to us. How we act on this information is entirely up to us. But we cannot lose because the Creator loves each one of us as if there was only one of us. Yesterday is gone, tomorrow doesn't exist – we need to accept Now. To accept, because only to want good karma to come our way is not to learn, but to allow our personalities to prevent our souls supporting, guiding and serving our needs.

Every karmic experience leaves an impression on our soul. When this happens the bridge of learning is crossed and we then allow our soul to serve us by moving us to the next karmic experience. If we trust our Maker and open our hearts to love, we will learn divine acceptance. This is what Jesus meant by 'turn the other cheek'. Do not worry about the future.

Whatever you need you will be guided to. If you give generously and help others to prosper, you will prosper. It may not seem obvious to you because we have personalities and egos that interfere. Release all fear and doubt, and when you lie down tonight before you go to sleep, say "I accept every minute and I will live it to the full to the best of my ability".

If you open the window in your heart to allow love to flow in, the freedom is indescribable and will guide you for all your days. If you mistrust what our Creator has in store, you will experience mistrust towards others and from others. Everything you do to others, you are actually doing to yourself, because karma will make you play out the situation again.

Acceptance is the key to your identity. This is true for all of us. This harmony is the inner peace that comes as you realise that all you need to survive will be drawn to you. You will all see with a new clarity, and so you will be able to solve problems with ease. Life will be wonderful. Leave the past and negative issues behind, and focus on all you believe to be good.

In the light of this truth, we will build our new planet. Keep this vision always in your sights and love your opposition unconditionally.

The message is: Love life and help others to love life. Be happy and make others happy. This is somewhat preferable, I would suggest, to what we see around us today. It is not an environmental crisis that we have first and foremost, nor a crisis of injustice, nor of peace, nor of cruelty. They are the by-products of the real crisis that faces us – the crisis of the human spirit. We will only solve those ills if we remove the cause of them, and the cause is that the spiritual truths that hold all the answers have been lost.

This can be seen clearly in the way we see people: not by what they are, but by what they own; not by how they care, but by what they wear; not by the size of their heart, but the size of their house. They have become the collective status symbols of the culture that controls the world, a culture that turns out more suicide, drug-taking, alcoholism and violence in all its forms and manifestations every year. A spiritual renaissance is long overdue.

The changes unfolding in this decade had to come, not only because the next stage of evolution is due, but to save us from ourselves. The alternative was the elimination of the planet well within the lifetimes of people alive today. Instead we are being offered a way out of the mess we have engineered, and our guides are the spiritual truths we have long forgotten.

By the time you read this, my consciousness will have been expanded further and I might know and understand more, but for now I can only say that the earth and humanity are in the process of transformation and we are being lifted as gently as possible to the next rung of evolution. It will not be without its many upsets and difficulties as we climb the last few steps, but the potential is there for a new and glorious tomorrow if we choose to take it.

The true potential of the Aquarian age will not be realised within the physical lifetimes of those on Earth today. The age won't be in its prime until at least the year 2500, and we will have to reincarnate to savour the full benefit of what we are about to do. But we can build the foundations for those who will follow us and we can watch the old delusions fading into history as we view creation with a new wonder and understanding. In the new age we will have the power to create the new Atlantis, and we will be given tremendous help and support from the entire solar system and beyond.

They will pass on to us, through thought-forms, the means to develop the new technologies. This is what I call 'the Eureka Factor' because thought-forms from the forces of Light and darkness are a source of our technological inspiration. We will also be able to manifest and de-manifest matter through sound. We will be able to levitate. We will use telepathy as we now use the telephone. There will be communication with the animals, devas and extra-terrestrials. Healing will be by natural methods and we will have little need for surgery. Colours are energy-frequencies, and as the vibrations quicken so the colours will become sharper, more brilliant, and there will be more shades. We will have more sounds for our music. There will be no need to use fossil fuels as we discover other sources of energy. The list goes on and on, and all of it can be ours.

But even as the new vibrations are phased in and attitudes change, I know that what I have said in these ten chapters will be met with much laughter, ridicule and condemnation. I have been left in no doubt whatsoever about the scale of the opposition I will face. I knew that when I began, and I am prepared for whatever may come. I do ask, however, that these words be met with open eyes and open hearts. No one is saying you must believe them. The traditional churches have put forward their view for 1500 years and they have every right to do so. I am offering another view; people must decide which they choose to believe.

Martin Luther King said that unarmed truth was the most powerful force in the universe, and he was right. You have been reading the first instalment of that unarmed truth. As the energies increase their tempo and our consciousness is raised to new heights, the basis of what I have said will be the conventional wisdom before too many years have passed. When that becomes the case, the fear of death will be replaced by the love of life, and as the darkness gives way to Light, the human race will enter adulthood and the Earth shall smile again. In the words of the poet, Shelley:

> A brighter dawn awaits the human day,
> When poverty and wealth, the thirst of fame,
> The fear of infamy, disease and woe,
> War with its million horrors and fierce hell,
> Shall live, but in the memory of time.

That dawn is set before us in the Aquarian age, and we can make that dream reality. We can replace suffering with joy, sadness with laughter, the emptiness of materialism with a new spiritual vision. We will have the power and the means to do each of these things if we want them badly enough. All we have to do is open our minds, open our hearts, and tune into the new tomorrow. We have been the lost sons and daughters of the Divine Family for long enough. It is time to go home.

Notes

(1) For those particularly interested in healing, *Vibrational Medicine* by Richard Gerber MD: Bear and Co, USA.

(2) See Prof. Fida Hassnain's *A Search for the Historical Jesus*: Gateway Books, 1993.

(3) I have used the name berkelium because that is the nearest chemical element to the one being introduced to the core. Berkelium was so named because it was prepared and identified at the radiation laboratory at the University of California at Berkeley in 1949. It was thought to be a human-made substance, but, apparently, something close to it occurs naturally within the earth. I use the name berkelium in that context. The iron will be fully replaced by the berkelium by early in the next century, but the poles will shift at the point when the negative energy-particles of berkelium overtake the influence of the positive iron. The Earth-spirit is responsible for controlling the balancing act, and how well this is done will decide if the etheric pole shift and axis tilt will be in 1994 or 95, and the physical in 98 or 99, said the communication. We were told that the scale of the axis tilt had been halved because of a 60% improvement in human consciousness between 1986 and 1990. This was a 60% improvement for humanity as a whole and not every individual. Some had made rapid progress while others had hardly moved. This new awareness and concern for the planet had, through the thought-energy it produced, strengthened the emotional health of the Earth enough to ensure the axis movement would be less than originally expected.

(4) The address for Fountain International is: PO Box 52, Torquay, Devon TQ2 8PE (stamped addressed envelope please).